THE PEOPLE SIDE OF PROJECT MANAGEMENT

To my parents, Arnold and Philomena – RLK
To my parents, Louis and Freda – ISL

THE PEOPLE SIDE OF PROJECT MANAGEMENT

WITHDRAWN

**Ralph L Kliem and
Irwin S Ludin**

Gower

First published in hardback 1992 by Gower Publishing.
Reprinted 1994

This paperback edition published 1995 by
Gower Publishing
Gower House
Croft Road
Aldershot
Hants. GU11 3HR
England

Gower
Old Post Road
Brookfield
Vermont 05036
USA

CIP catalogue records for this book are available from the British Library

ISBN 0 566 07363 3 (Hbk)
    0 566 07668 3 (Pbk)

Printed in Great Britain at the University Press, Cambridge

Table of Contents

v

List of Figures

Introduction

Throughout the history of project management, project managers have managed their projects according to three criteria: cost, schedule, and quality (see Figure I.1). They treated all other considerations as subordinate.

Ironically, following this approach has not proven too successful for any of the three criteria. Projects in most industries often exceed project completion dates by months, even years,

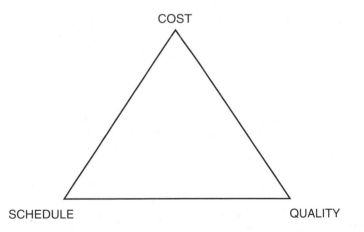

COST

SCHEDULE   QUALITY

Figure I.1   *Traditional three criteria for managing projects*

and overrun their budgets by thousands, even millions, of dollars.

In addition, each criterion seems to go in different directions. Meeting the schedule often means foregoing budget and quality considerations. Adhering to budget frequently means sacrificing quality or ignoring the schedule. Concentrating on quality means 'blowing' the budget or ignoring the schedule.

All this has occurred when project managers have a wide array of project management tools and techniques at their disposal. Many plan their projects by developing work breakdown structures, time estimates, and network diagrams. Many organize their projects by developing organization charts and forms and allocating resources. Many control their projects by collecting information on progress of the project and developing contingency plans, to address anticipated problems. In addition, these tools and techniques have become more sophisticated and automated.

Then why the dismal record, at least from the perspective of the three criteria?

The answer is that schedule, budget, and quality are not enough. One other important criterion is missing: people.

What many project managers fail to realize is that their handling of people affects the outcome of their projects. Indeed, their neglect or mismanagement of people can affect schedule, cost, and quality.

People management, therefore, is as important for managing a project as schedule, budget, and quality. Indeed, it can bridge the gap that often exists between the other three criteria (see Figure I.2).

Successful project managers are those who recognize the importance of people in completing their projects. They know that without people no project would exist in the first place. They also recognize that people play an integral role in completing the project within budget, on schedule, and with top workmanship.

The people side of project management views people as a critical factor in completing projects and recognizes that handling human beings cannot occur in a mechanical, systems-oriented way.

In contrast, the 'hardside' of project management entails

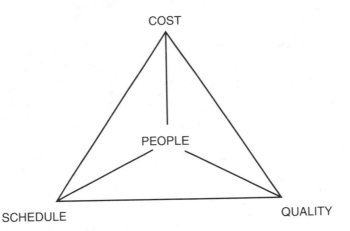

Figure I.2 *Contemporary four criteria for managing projects*

planning projects by developing work breakdown structures, network diagrams, and budgets; organizing by developing organization charts and forms as well as allocating resources; and, controlling by collecting information on progress of the project and developing contingency plans to address antici-pated problems.

The people side is not more important than the hardside and vice versa. Rather project managers must recognize the equal importance of both sides. That entails adding the fourth important criterion, people, to the traditional three: costs, schedule, and quality.

PART I

The world of project management

Chapter 1

The major players

To progress smoothly, project management requires that four key players (shown in Figure 1.1) participate. These players are the project manager, senior management, client, and the project team.

Project manager

As a project manager you play a vital function in the entire project. You are the one who is responsible for the successful execution of your project. That can only occur if you take the lead in getting all parties to participate fully in their projects. You serve as a bridge between all three parties, enabling communication between senior management, the client, and the project team. When any one party fails to participate in the project, you fail. The communication breakdowns that occur will lead to obstacles towards making any progress.

Project managers are crucial to a successful project for another obvious reason. They are the ones responsible for managing the entire project. They are the people who plan, organize, control, and lead it. If project managers fail to participate fully in their projects, the likelihood of failure increases.

Some project managers do not participate in a project even though they hold the title of 'project manager.' They may be uninterested in the project because it was forced upon them or they assumed the position by circumstance. In response to this

PROJECT MANAGER

- Orchestrates successful delivery of the project
- Enables interactive communications among senior management, client, and project team
- Coordinates effective and efficient participation
- Develops project plans, including estimates, work breakdown structure, and schedules
- Provides mechanism for monitoring and tracking progress regarding schedule, budget, and technical performance
- Creates infrastructure for managing the project team

SENIOR MANAGEMENT

- Determine project's fate (proceed or stop)
- Allocate project support resources including money and manpower
- Identify favoured or preferred projects
- Continued participation throughout the life cycle
- Provide strategic guidance and direction

CLIENT

- Pays for the project/product
- Coordinates with project manager for project/product clarification
- Uses the product
- Approves the product
- Dedicates resources to the project including people, time, and money
- Communicates requirements

PROJECT TEAM

- Supports the project manager
- Provides requisite skills and creativity
- Operates as a unified team
- Works with the client to obtain requirements, feedback, and approvals

Figure 1.1   *Responsibilities of four key players in projects*

situation, they may fail to plan, organize, control, or lead these projects adequately. The results are unsuccessful projects, that is, projects that fail to meet goals and objectives with regard to cost, schedule, and quality.

As a side note, the notion that management is nonproductive is incorrect in today's environment, especially in service industries like data processing. Frederick Taylor, the father of scientific management, established the idea that management and labour work together like a team – their ultimate goal being the success of the corporation. In those days (the 1880s), management had been traditionally viewed as being nonproductive; however, in environments where specialization is prevalent, poor management can result in poor productivity. The project manager of today plays an important central role in ensuring that communication and coordination among different participants occur efficiently and effectively. If project managers fail to perform such tasks disaster is soon forthcoming.

Senior management

The project manager needs the participation of senior management because much power resides with them. Senior management decide whether the project will proceed. They also determine the extent of support the project will receive relative to other projects. If they do not view the project as having much importance, senior management will allocate resources to more 'significant' endeavours. If they have a favourable view, the opposite will occur.

The importance of senior management's participation becomes very clear when there is a split over how important a project is. This may give a project a 'stop and go' mode of operation which can result in poor productivity and low morale. The problem can become even worse if management withdraws their support.

For example, senior management may waiver in support of a project due to changing market conditions. One month they support the project; the next month they give priority attention to another one. People with special skills may be pulled from the original project and then sent to another and returned. As a result the employees start feeling insignificant rather than contributing members of the company.

Senior management's participation is critical but what is even more important is the style of participation. If they participate in an overbearing, authoritative manner, senior management may constrain the project manager and, consequently, the project. Senior management must do what they do best – manage. They should not tell members of the team how to do their jobs. If senior management want the project to succeed they must allow the project manager and team members the latitude to do the job. That means delegating, something many senior managers fail to do.

Senior management must not, however, adopt a policy of benign neglect. They must keep abreast of what occurs on the project. The emphasis is on *what*, not *how*. Feedback up and down the chain of command is absolutely essential.

Client

The client is the reason why the project exists in the first place. Clients may be internal or external (outside the company). They pay for the project, either at the beginning or later. Their participation, like that of senior management, is principally during the start and end of a project.

The client is not always a monolithic entity but may comprise several types of people. First, there are the people who pay for the product; they typically are the principal decision-makers. Second, there are the people whose function is the coordination with the project manager during most of the project; they are the main contacts for information and clarification. Third, and finally, there are the people who will use the product in their operational environment; they see the value of the product in terms of how it improves their productivity.

Dealing with the client requires sensitivity. What and how much to tell a client depends on your relationship. The best policy, from your perspective as a project manager, is to maintain an open and honest relationship. Any hint of dishonesty or duplicity can result in a breakdown of communications and a cancellation of agreements.

There is another aspect to the requirement for sensitivity.

Because the client is not always monolithic, project managers can find themselves caught in a political crossfire. They can make one person on the client's side happy and inadvertently anger someone else. Project managers must always be aware of this possibility and focus on the key participants (in respect to political power) in the client's organization.

Project team

These people comprise the project manager's team and their skills should complement one another.

Unity and cooperation among team members are absolutely necessary. Projects involve a diverse number of specialized skills which must complement one another in achieving goals. If team members fight with one another, energy is directed into unproductive endeavours. If the team members fight with the client, the latter can withhold cooperation, or, worse, cancel the contract. If team members fight with senior management, communications up and down the chain of command suffer and so, ultimately, will productivity.

Without the support of any one of these people, the quality of the product will decline.

As the project manager, you play an important role in ensuring that senior management, client, and project team contribute to your project. If your relationship with them deteriorates in any way or if their relationships with one another worsens, the people side of project management can prove very difficult and damage progress, affecting schedule, budget, and workmanship.

Chapter 2

What happens when the people side is overlooked

Perhaps the best way to see what is meant by the people side of project management is to regard a project as a system. That means seeing a project as consisting of different components interacting with one another in various degrees.

Components of a system

A project is a system in which these components (see Figure 2.1) interact with one another either directly or indirectly. A component can be an actor, function, policy, procedure, goal, or requirement. Each component performs a significant function.

The actors or key players in a project are the client, senior management, project manager, and team. Each one contributes to the successful execution of a project and can take many forms.

In some environments, for example, more than one project manager exists, where one person manages the business aspects and the other manages the technical area.

The project team often contains a 'core' group of people and a supporting group. The former consists of the people who have the skills required to plan and organize the project. They may have either the essential business or technical skills or both. The latter is composed of people who become

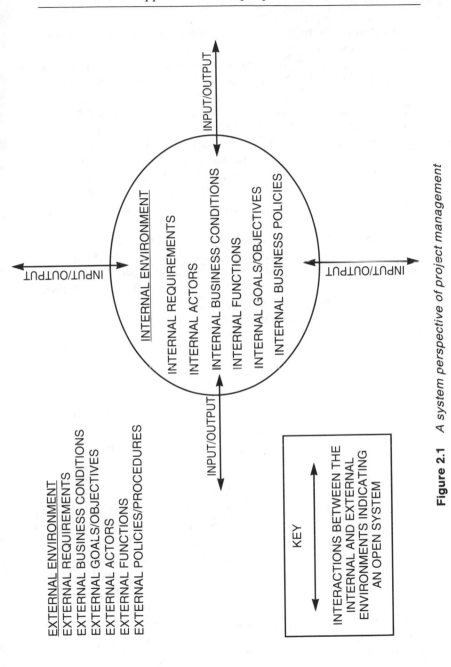

Figure 2.1 *A system perspective of project management*

involved once the project has been planned and organized and is ready to begin.

The client, too, might consist of several people. These may include liaison analysts, coordinators, operators, and various members of management.

The internal functions, or subsystems, are innumerable, some being more significant than others. The four fundamental functions are planning, organizing, controlling, and leading. Each one of these can be further divided into subfunctions. For example, you could subdivide planning into preparing a statement of work and building a work breakdown structure. You could explode each one into further subfunctions, or subsystems.

Internal policies and procedures regulate the behaviour of a system. They determine under what circumstances the actors and functions, for instance, can occur and interact with one another. These policies and procedures can either be formal or informal. Formal means hard copy, promulgated documents specifying philosophy and the steps for implementing it. Informal means modes of behaviour are not officially announced but are very present nonetheless, such as how often to take a break from the job.

Many environments, for example, have a methodology for managing projects. This methodology covers all or most aspects of a project's life cycle. However, many organizations fail to document the methodology. Even if they do document it, many others do not enforce it; they prefer to call it a guideline rather than a standard.

Internal requirements are the minimum levels of support to make the system operational. You must have, for instance, minimum levels of time, money, and labour. All systems require a minimum resource level to avoid dysfunctional behaviour (see Figure 2.2).

Many support functions within a company, such as engineering and data processing, continually face this problem because they may develop products for one or more clients. They need to charge for their work via a chargeback system. Unless clients provide a satisfactory level of payment for that work then the support function will have to reprioritize projects and scale down efforts.

- Lack of enthusiasm
- Lack of respect
- Lack of management commitment
- Lack of challenging work
- Lack of workable operating procedures
- Ill-defined statement of work
- Duplication of effort
- Poor communication skills
- Inattentive listening
- Lack of incentives
- Undefined deliverables
- Poor work environment
- Lack of tools to do my job
- Resource poor

Figure 2.2 *Characteristics of dysfunctional behaviour*

All systems exist to achieve specific goals and objectives; they are purposeful. All functions, actors, requirements, policies, procedures, goals, and objectives are the 'tools' for the system to meet its purpose. In the construction industry, the goal is to build a structure, whether a house, building, or stadium. In data processing, it is to deliver a software product. In aerospace, it is an aeroplane or missile.

The internal actors, functions, policies, procedures, goals, objectives, and requirements all interact with one another either directly or indirectly. For example, each actor performs one or more functions that will achieve goals and objectives. Policies and procedures and minimum requirements will determine the extent to which the actors can perform their applicable functions.

On a construction project, for instance, the field engineers work with the mechanical engineers and the superintendent; the superintendent coordinates the work with the project manager as well as with field accountants, supervisors, and subcontractors. All this activity occurs under some *modus operandi* whether formal or informal.

Sometimes these elements will conflict with one another. For example, an internal actor does not perform a function or does but not at the desired level. This lack may be due to a lack of resources or poorly formulated policies or procedures.

Internal conflict then occurs because other actors are not receiving a satisfactory output to do their job.

You would be mistaken, however, to assume that the internal elements interact only with one another. Often these elements not only interact with each other internally but also with those located in the environment external to the system. Most systems are open systems, that is, they are not self-contained. Projects in the pharmaceutical industry, for example, may develop a drug that will eventually need approval from a government institution prior to release to the public. In this case, the firm is not totally self-contained because it must interact with an entity outside its boundary – the government institution.

Hence, a system may have a boundary that defines its borders but does not totally exclude any contact with the external environment. Inputs and outputs enter and leave the system, thereby creating an open rather than closed environment. The elements entering and leaving may be goals and objectives, minimum requirements, or policies and procedures set either by higher management or some higher level. A closed system, however, does not allow interaction between its internal environment and the external environment. Likewise, external elements cannot influence internal ones.

Disequilibrium defined

Disequilibrium can occur when the internal environment and the external environment conflict with one another. This conflict can originate either from within the system or its external environment. For example, the goals and objectives set by the external environment may be too ambitious because the system lacks the requisite number of actors or the internal minimum requirements are too low.

A prime internal source of disequilibrium on projects is the emphasis on the technical side of project management rather than the people side. Project managers often concentrate on developing or revising schedules or the budget, developing or revising processes, or introducing new tools and techniques to improve quality. Addressing all these areas is important. What often happens, however, is that project managers fail to address the people side. Improved schedules, better tools, and more money either do not dramatically alter the circumstances or where they do alter the circumstances, the effect is less due to the presence of people problems on the project. Even if the problems are overcome, the long term effects on the existing staff could prove more costly than the effort expended to improve performance regarding schedule, costs, and quality.

An example of a system

The following example of a new automobile project presents the systems perspective.

You have been appointed the project manager for a project that will result in developing a four-door saloon car that provides the latest digital technology for the driver. You need to determine what you want to achieve and develop 'measuring sticks' to assess how well you are achieving your goal. These are your internal goals and objectives. Then you need to decide the tasks required to make the project a success. These are your internal functions. You know that certain functions are more important than others.

Knowing the internal goals, objectives, and functions of your project, you can begin determining the internal minimum requirements to complete it. Typically, that involves deciding the time, people, material, and equipment needed to complete the project.

You can then develop internal policies and procedures for managing the project. These might address areas like the conduct and schedule of meetings, methods for collecting information on progress of the project, and procedures for change control.

Your project does not, however, operate in a vacuum. You know that you will face pressures from the external environment. Your senior management, for instance, may say that you will receive less money than you need. Or they may impose policies and procedures that restrict your control of the project.

You can either comply with those requirements or not.

Either way, you may face conflict that will result in disequilibrium.

You may decide to take the first choice, complying with the requirements. Certain actors on the project may have to perform specific functions under a severe time constraint, possibly resulting in unsatisfactory performance. Other actors using that output may be unable to perform their functions because of unsatisfactory support. Internal conflict, or disequilibrium, could result.

Or you may decide to take the second choice, not complying with those requirements. This decision can lead to conflict with the external environment, perhaps with your senior management or with the client. The problem may not just occur there, either. Conflict with the external environment can lead to conflict in the internal environment. For instance, your senior management may make decisions that can upset existing policies and procedures, causing conflict among different actors and influencing the level of performance for each function. They may decide to lower the priority of your project and allocate your resources to more important ones. Under these circumstances, disequilibrium can result.

Not easy

As a project manager you have an important responsibility. You must adopt an appropriate management style in the face of a myriad of circumstances, ranging from legal to personnel matters. Your project can go awry for countless reasons. The environment is susceptible to influences, some positive and some negative, from the project's internal or external environments.

You can see, therefore, that taking an integrated approach to project management is important. Too often, project managers take only one perspective, usually the hardside. They either overlook or ignore other critical areas such as the people side. In a sense, they are like a racehorse wearing blinkers: they can focus on only one thing. The result is a project plagued with serious problems. The project managers are always on the defensive, constantly trying to deal with one crisis after another. As a result, they and their team become so weakened that the project falls further behind in almost every conceivable category.

Chapter 3

The dynamic world of projects from a people perspective

All projects go through several stages, rather like a human being. They also go through phases. Within each stage and phase a series of people side issues arise that can affect the relationships among the four parties (project manager, senior management, client, and project team) as well as the outcome.

Stages of a project

All projects are systems that proceed through several stages, from the moment of their inception to their discontinuation. These basic stages, shown in Figure 3.1, are gestation, growth, independence, decline, and death.

Gestation

This stage entails the birth of a project. Principal parties in an organization recognize that something has gone astray with the current operational mode. Perhaps the volume of business is too much to handle or the competitive market requires a new faster, better way to handle business. Whatever the reason, the need for a project arises.

At first, the justification for the project goes through a tough fight. More questions than answers arise and certain

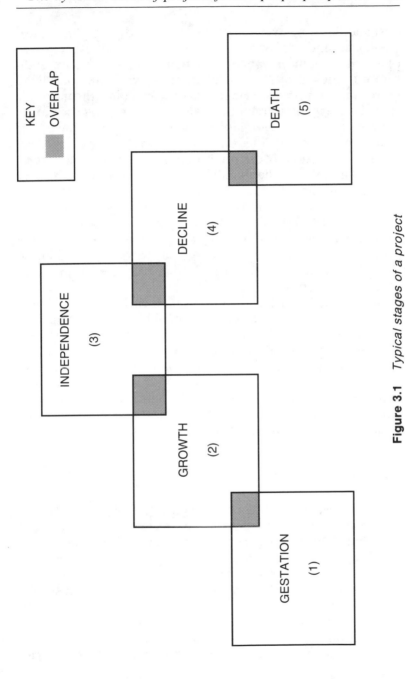

Figure 3.1 *Typical stages of a project*

obstacles must be overcome. The 'old guard' wants to protect the current mode of operation and will try to squash any idea of a project. Some members of management fear that expenditure on a new project will detract from what are considered more important areas. Hence, a project going through this stage is struggling to retain its existence and gain acceptance. People's attitudes, the organizational arrangement, the power structure, and many other factors stand in the way of a project coming to fruition. More often than not, the obstacles are so overwhelming that the likelihood of a project going beyond this stage is minimal.

From a human relations standpoint this stage of a project is the most vulnerable. People – client, team members, and the project manager – must have a feeling of trust and unity if the project is to proceed smoothly. All parties must be willing to share knowledge, skill, time, and other resources to plan and organize the project.

The client, lacking trust among its members and with the team, may begin to quarrel. They could start bickering over the requirements or fail to share information. The team members might start 'doing their own thing' without really understanding the requirements or goal of the project. Indeed, they may ignore, or fight with, the client. The project manager, especially in a matrix environment, may start haggling for control over resources, frequently people, with functional managers who may have different priorities.

Growth

This is the next stage that a project enters, if all goes well in the gestation stage. Here, the project earns legitimacy. That is, it has gained acceptance by the decision-makers and has a credible justification for its existence. It can now compete with existing projects for resources.

The growth stage, like the gestation one, is not an easy one. A project in this stage will be competing against more established projects for finite resources, which can include money, time, labour, equipment, facilities, or anything else.

Regardless of the competition, however, the project can

only proceed according to the mission and rules established by the decision-makers. Quite often, the rules are stacked in favour of older projects, thereby making it difficult for the new project to grow. 'Growing pains' can result. Other projects may win more of the finite resources. They may even try to destroy the new project by denying the growing project critical information or trying to steal its people.

If the project survives such competition, it can look forward to the next stage.

Ideally, everyone in a project cooperates. The client, team, and project manager will have resolved their differences among themselves and between each other. The client sees the value of the project and will pay accordingly for the product. The team feels that it has a purpose, or mission, that will do itself, the client, and the company some good. The project manager now feels in control of the direction of the project.

However, disequilibrium may arise at this stage too. Team members might feel that other teams are using more state-of-the-art tools and receiving privileges to which they, too, are entitled; in fact, team members may feel that way among themselves. The technical members and the non-technical ones might feel they are not getting the support that they need to do their job. The client, too, might start squabbling among its constituents, especially if they are supporting several projects. Their money, time, and people become limited in their availability. The client starts vacillating over priorities which contributes to the team's frustration. The project manager is now sandwiched between two unhappy groups – the team and client. Potentially, communications can plummet among all participants.

Independence

Here the project becomes self-sustaining; it can compete with relative equality with the other projects. It has the resources required to complete the job and progress is being made towards reaching the goals and objectives.

Typically, the project has senior management supporters who protect it and give it the support necessary for completion. It becomes an integral part of the organization with the project manager participating in key decisions affecting its outcome, something that may or may not occur in the growth stage. As the independence stage concludes, the project starts declining.

Most projects reaching this stage have few serious people problems. The client supports the project because its discontented members have conceded or departed. Team members feel they can complete the project because they have a good rapport with the client and with fellow team members and have management support. The project manager feels in control of all aspects of the project.

Although reaching this stage is an accomplishment in itself, disequilibrium can arise here too. The client might feel that they can interfere with the technical and managerial aspects of the project. Their participation might threaten the team's autonomy. Representatives from the client might, for example, insist on approaching product design in a certain way now that they feel comfortable with the team. Team members might resent such intrusions and start ignoring client input. They might also start feeling that their work has become routine and that they are stagnating; such sentiments can lead to disgruntlement and departure. The project manager might become 'political' now that the project has technical matters under control and this can impair his judgement. The project manager could also stagnate along with the team members due to over-confidence; indeed, workmanship, budget, and schedule could all start declining. Everyone involved in the project starts acquiring an arrogance that can lead to severe people problems.

Declining

In this stage, the project winds down. Its main activities have been completed, and there is now difficulty in justifying its existence. Either the project is successful in delivering the final product or management feels that the advantages of the project no longer exist. Whatever the reason, the project must fight for the support and visibility it enjoyed in the independence stage. In the eyes of senior management, the project no longer has legitimacy, since the major goals have been reached or are no longer relevant. Management may now view other projects as being more important.

In any case, other projects will start receiving a greater share of the resources and attention. Some may 'steal' resources, whether money or people, from the project as it becomes subordinate to other projects. After time, the project goes into the final stage.

People side issues often surface during this stage. That is because everyone sees the end coming. If the project has been less than satisfactory, the client may start blaming its members or the project team for the poor results and vice versa. The project manager can find it difficult to retain people, either because many transferred or because management deems their services more valuable elsewhere. Remaining team members may reduce their performance knowing that whatever they do will not make a difference or spend their time looking for another position.

If the project has a satisfactory conclusion (such as a successful delivery of the product) all participants will feel euphoric, like winners. Shifting the blame is virtually non-existent as everyone seeks to identify themselves with the project.

Project managers can reduce the likelihood of much dysfunctional behaviour by emphasizing the importance of people's contributions to the completion of the project and the project's contribution to the company's goals. They must also work to keep the client involved. Project managers must at least communicate the importance of staying the course.

Death

In this stage, the project rapidly declines in favour with decision-makers. The reason may be that the project is completed, or may need to be redeveloped (for example due to its age or a changing environment), is not delivering a quality product, or has depleted funding. Whatever the reason, the project has little or no legitimacy for its existence. Management then decides to terminate the project by reducing resources, such as money, rather than sustain it.

The death of a project can come rapidly, after any stage. It is most susceptible, however, immediately after the gestation stage. Projects at that point struggle to gain acceptance. If they fail, they will lose their support from management and become non-existent.

All projects end. They might end successfully, for example by delivering a quality product on schedule and within budget. They might end due to a lack of money, time, or talent. They might end due to politics. Whatever the reason, people problems are not significant unless the people on the project will suffer from the stigma of having worked on a failure, or, as they go to another project, their morale is so low as to affect their output.

To avoid such dysfunctional behaviour, the project manager can make an effort to help remaining team members find work that will be rewarding. In addition, project managers can solicit input from team members on why the project failed and for ideas on how to avoid a similar catastrophe in the future.

Each stage contains the 'seeds' of the succeeding stage. The elements of the growth stage are within the gestation stage. For example, a project in the gestation stage can have elements of legitimacy; management may overtly endorse the project and recognize its importance immediately.

Phases of a project

Every project goes through a series of phases as well as stages. These phases are: feasibility, formulation, implementation, installation, and sustaining. Their relationship to one another is shown in Figure 3.2. Each one has its own set of people side issues.

Feasibility

In this phase, management determines whether the project is a practical alternative to the current mode of operation; in other

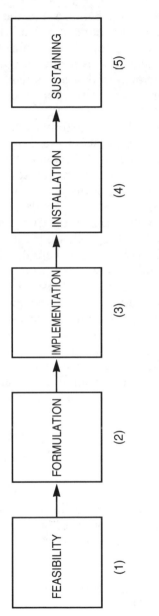

Figure 3.2 *Typical phases of a project*

words, will the project prove beneficial to the company? Management conducts a preliminary study of the requirements, costs, and operational concerns and makes a 'go/no go' decision. If management makes a negative decision, it drops the project. If management makes a positive one, it authorizes funds and other support and gives permission to move to the next phase.

All projects go through the feasibility phase. At the conclusion of the phase, some projects die while others proceed. During this phase, people problems can arise that can affect the degrees of success in subsequent phases.

Members of the client faction may start conflicting over whether a computing solution is feasible or worthwhile. The old guard (those protecting the status quo) and the new guard (those favouring a change) may clash. If the conflict continues rather than reaching consensus, then it will emerge again during other critical moments of the project.

Team members performing the feasibility study could find themselves being attacked by both the client and their colleagues. Their morale could plummet, especially if they perceive any lack of support from management.

The project manager could also feel pressure from the management to justify the project, or might become embroiled in the politics of the client's environment. Either way, the project manager's ability to manage will be hard-pressed, and may even deteriorate.

Formulation

The project team defines in detail the needs and wants of the client by receiving and documenting current business activities. The team then develops alternative solutions to meet those wants and needs. It selects the best alternative and develops detailed plans to implement it.

In the formulation phase, the project manager faces a similar set of people side issues. Members of the client faction may haggle over requirements and if consensus is not reached then progress in subsequent phases can prove difficult and affect the design of a product. Team members may find themselves frustrated with the indecisiveness of the client and fail to capture requirements completely. The project manager then has to try to keep the lines of communication open between the team and the client.

Implementation

In this phase, the actual building of the product occurs, expending considerable resources, such as time and labour. The team constructs all the main components and ensures that everything works harmoniously. The team performs extensive testing on the product to make sure that it is operational and addresses the needs and wants of the client.

Quite often, the effects of people side issues in the previous stages (feasibility and formulation) emerge in this phase. The people problems in the feasibility phase might affect how much resources, such as money or equipment, the client wants to expend on the project. The people side issues in the formulation phase might influence how well the system being built meets requirements.

Common people side issues in this phase include erratic workloads (such as dramatic low and high periods of effort), overtime, burnout, frustration, and tension. The client often does not participate in this phase. The project team, especially the technical members, plays the central role. They build the product that was defined in the feasibility and formulation stages. The project manager must work to keep the team working cost-effectively with high morale.

Installation

This is the phase when the product is operational in the client's environment. Theoretically it meets all the specifications of the client and is delivered with all accompanying material.

The project manager must handle this phase carefully. The reason is that the client may have high expectations about the product. From the client's perspective, the product should be an asset rather than a liability. If the product fails or the installation proves too disruptive, the client's attitude towards the product and the project quickly deteriorates.

In this phase, therefore, the project manager's focus shifts from the project team (though still important) to the client. The project manager must deliver a product that the client will not only accept but use in its daily operations.

The project manager must ensure that communication continues between the team and the client. If the client finds something unsatisfactory during acceptance testing, the project manager must decide whether it is a valid objection.

Sometimes, people side issues surface. Client and team members may disagree, even argue, over whether the system meets the requirements. The client may feel pressure to accept the system because team members want to work on other projects. Team members may feel that the client is nit-picking.

Sustaining

Following installation, the client now has direct control over the product, using it daily. The experience can range from being totally pleasant to one that can result in a project manager's tarnished reputation. Quite often problems with the product surface in this phase. Some problems will be minor while others are more serious.

Ideally, the sustaining phase should proceed as smoothly as possible. Note, however, that the more complex the final product the greater the expense during the sustaining phase.

In data processing, for example, the sustaining phase of a project can comprise from 60 to 80 per cent of the total cost of a product.

Whether the experience is smooth or difficult, the project manager provides ongoing support to the client, and may also revise the product to meet the customer's needs.

In the sustaining phase, the project is no longer just that – a project. The system continues running but the user receives maintenance support from a different group of people.

These five phases – feasibility, formulation, implementation, installation, and sustaining – do not necessarily appear serially; that is, one finishes and then the next one begins. Two or more of these phases can occur concurrently. For example, the implementation phase can start when approximately half of the formulation phase is completed. The installation phase can begin when two-thirds of the implementation phase is done. The obvious advantage to this arrangement is that it shortens the life of a project. A law of diminishing returns, however, applies to running the phases concurrently. Burnout of key employees, excessive overtime, and high labour costs can result.

Fast-tracking

Under some circumstances, projects are fast-tracked, meaning the project goes through each phase, but at a faster pace than normally expected, and at a reduced cost.

Fast-tracking works best when the goals and objectives of a project are clearly defined. For research and development environments that create state-of-the-art software, for example, fast-tracking does not work very successfully. For constructing an office building, which requires many straightforward tasks and a clear goal, fast-tracking often works well. It works well, too, if the project team, in addition to having a clear goal, has experience of working with one another and each person knows his or her job well. Otherwise, fast-tracking may serve as an excuse to ignore the important functions of planning, organizing, controlling, and leading a project.

If you elect to use fast-tracking on a project, remember that it is not an excuse for skipping any of the phases of a project. It simply means that you will conduct some phases at an accelerated pace. Neither is it an excuse to exceed budget estimates, slide the schedule, or develop products, such as documentation, of poor quality.

Mixing the phases and stages of projects

In the first section of this chapter, you learned about the different stages of a project. In the second section, you read about the different phases of a project. Both can exist simultaneously under varying circumstances (see Figure 3.3).

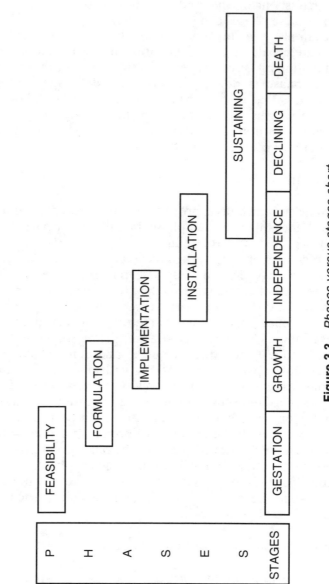

Figure 3.3 *Phases versus stages chart*

A project may exist in the gestation phase for a long time but may be in the implementation phase. That is because of a lack of support for the project, either by senior management or even the client. The project manager may still be trying to justify the project.

A project may be in the growth stage even while simultaneously in the implementation phase. In this case, senior management recognize the importance of the project and one willing to allocate whatever resources are required for its successful conclusion. They may even expand the project's purview. The project may start having all the features of a programme due to its level of magnitude relative to other projects. It receives more than all the resources it needs to succeed while other projects are neglected.

A project may be in the independence stage while in the sustaining phase. Because the project was so successful, senior management and the client are willing to treat the continued support of the product in the sustaining phase as an 'ongoing' endeavour that has the same level of status as a project in the earlier phases.

A project may be in the decline stage, regardless of phase. Senior management may feel that more important projects exist that demand attention. They may also decide to trim existing resources. The project quickly loses legitimacy.

A project may be in the death stage during any phase. Management make the decision to cut all support and the project becomes non-existent.

PART II

People and projects

Chapter 4

The people side of planning

A good project plan is the core of project management (see Figure 4.1). It serves as the roadmap or gameplan for completing the project on time and within budget. A high correlation exists between the failure to have good project plans and not managing a project cost-effectively.

To have good project plans requires the development of: statement of work (SOW), work breakdown structure (WBS), time estimates, and the schedule (see Figure 4.2). The process of developing each of these presents its own people side issues.

A good project plan:
- Is readable
- Is concise
- Is understandable
- Is current
- Has a staff and management signature block
- Incorporates revisions via formal procedure
- Designates responsibilities
- Defines interfaces with other systems and organizations
- Identifies all reviewers

Figure 4.1 *Characteristics of a good project plan*

37

- Executive summary
- Mission statement
- Scope
- Goals/objectives
- Deliverables (including statement of work and work breakdown structure)
- Constraints/Restrictions/Assumptions
- Roles and responsibilities (including organization chart)
- Cost/benefit analysis
- Schedule

Figure 4.2   *Typical topics covered in a project plan*

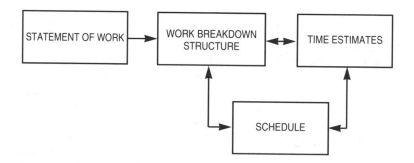

Figure 4.3   *The planning process*

Understanding the process

Before discussing these issues, an understanding of the sequence of development is necessary. The SOW, WBS, time estimates, and schedules are developed in that order (see Figure 4.3).

The statement of work is an agreement between the project manager and the client defining the final product and overall responsibilities as well as the budgetary, schedule, and technical constraints.

Using the information in the SOW, particularly the product description and the overall responsibilities, the project manager can develop the work breakdown structure. The WBS is a detailed listing of tasks required to produce the final product. Ideally, the WBS should have sufficient detail to enable tracking the level of completion for each task during the project.

Next, the project manager, receiving input from other people, compiles a time estimate to complete each task. These estimates not only indicate the amount of time needed to complete each task but calculate the dates for starting and finishing each one.

Using the work breakdown structure and time estimates the project manager can develop a schedule. First, he interconnects the tasks in the WBS to form a logical sequence. Then, using the time estimates, he calculates the start and stop dates for each task while considering any mandatory dates, such as for completing a task or the project by a specific date.

The people side of the statement of work

The statement of work is a document which serves as an agreement between the project manager, senior management, and client. It lists the goals and objectives of the project, the major responsibilities, the main deliverables and milestone dates, the methodology or approach, the constraints, and acceptance criteria (see Figure 4.4). Once the project begins, the SOW serves as the 'organic' document that directs subsequent actions. Any changes in the SOW must go through rigorous change control and must have the approval of all parties (see Figure 4.5).

While the idea behind a statement of work sounds easy, it becomes very complicated to execute when people become involved. Three parties (the client, senior management, and project manager) must agree to it (see Figure 4.6).

The client wants the SOW to protect its interests throughout the course of the project. It wants a high quality product at minimum cost, not at the cheapest price. It wants the product delivered on time using periodic benchmark dates as control. It also expects the organization's senior management to provide the necessary people and equipment to do the job.

Senior management want the project to meet the client's needs but not to the exclusion of other clients nor at the cost of the total budget. Above all, they want the client to realize

I. INTRODUCTION
    A. Project goal
    B. Objectives
    C. Scope
II. DELIVERABLES/PRODUCTS
    A. Software
    B. Hardware
    C. Training
    D. Documentation
    E. Support
III. CONSTRAINTS
    A. Schedule
    B. Budget
    C. Environmental
    D. Legal
IV. SCHEDULE
    A. Scheduling techniques
    B. Scheduling tools
    C. Status collection
    D. Status reporting
V. BUDGET
    A. Budget calculation techniques
    B. Budget status collection
    C. Budget status reporting
VI. ROLES AND RESPONSIBILITIES
    A. Client
    B. Project manager/team
    C. Reporting relationships
VII. REFERENCES
    A. Policies
    B. Procedures
    C. Statutes
VIII. ADDITIONAL CONSIDERATIONS
IX. SIGNATURES OF AGREEMENT

Figure 4.4   *Outline of a typical statement of work*

that the project involves the participation of everyone, not just themselves or the client.

The project manager, along with the project team, wants to complete the project with autonomy, with ample resources, and in a realistic time frame.

Of all three parties, the project manager suffers the greatest pressure. He must complete the project according to the SOW, otherwise, the client and senior manager may blame him for

- Understand exactly what the project will achieve and under what conditions, including goals, objectives, and constraints
- Regulate modifications to the statement of work through formal change control jurisdiction including schedule, budget, quality, and responsibilities
- Retain focus on the statement of work 'document' as a business contract
- Proper dissemination of copies of the statement of work to 'all' involved parties including management, client, programmers, analysts, administrators, and technical writers
- Ensure adherence to the provisions of the statement of work
- Ensure that the provisions of the statement of work comply with existing company policies and procedures

Figure 4.5   *Common statement of work concerns for the project manager, senior management, client, and project team*

not meeting the details of the agreement. The project manager, therefore, must make a realistic agreement that all three parties can accept. That is not easy when he has a client that wants the most for its money and senior management that wants the project.

Managing the people side of developing the SOW

To make the people side of developing the statement of work easier for yourself, you can take several actions. Recognize that all parties have an interest in the project and that the SOW must represent a compromise between those interests. Without that sense of compromise the project will be plagued with problems throughout. The client will claim that the product does not meet their needs and senior management will start looking to hold someone accountable for the sad state of affairs, meaning you, the project manager. The project team will also face productivity problems.

Never start any work on the project without executing a SOW. Everyone should understand exactly what the project will achieve and under what conditions. Without a SOW, the client will wonder what they are paying for, senior management will feel out of control, team members will not under-

PROJECT MANAGER

- Provides deliverables by milestone date
- Makes realistic agreement for acceptance of statement of work
- Identifies resources required
- Drafts statement of work
- Coordinates review and approval
- Co-signs statement of work
- Identifies and clarifies responsibilities
- Identifies constraints

SENIOR MANAGEMENT

- Co-sign statement of work
- Provide necessary resources for product delivery including labour, equipment, and budget

CLIENT

- Identifies goals and objectives
- Co-signs statement of work
- Outlines requirements and deliverables
- Provides budgetary and schedule limitations

PROJECT TEAM

- Identifies methodology, approach, and constraints
- Provides input to project manager

Figure 4.6 *Tasks/responsibilities regarding the statement of work*

stand what they are doing or why, and the project manager will face severe problems with all three parties.

Regulate modifications to the SOW, that is, place revisions to it under change control. Whether changes involve schedule, budget, quality, or responsibilities, each change must be tracked, analysed, and approved or disapproved. That process precludes subsequent charges that the SOW in spirit and letter has been violated. Once that happens fingerpointing becomes the primary activity, instead of developing the product.

- Develop an integrated payroll system
- Develop an inventory system having customized reports

The above examples have one thing in common – unclear ideas of what the project achieves. These unclear ideas include a lack of meaningful mission, scope, goals, objectives, and/or requirements.

A clearer approach might be:

- Develop an integrated payroll system including payroll, personnel, and benefits system.
- Develop an order inventory system to track and maintain customer inventory, order, and administrative functions and reports.

Figure 4.7 *Unclear ideas of what a project achieves*

Make sure that the SOW plays a significant role in all meetings between the client, senior management, and yourself. A tendency often exists for all parties to agree to a SOW and then manage the project with little or no reference to the document. The activities of the project stray from the goals and objectives, responsibilities, and other factors in the SOW. In the end the various parties start fingerpointing or expressing dissatisfaction with the product or the way the project has been managed (see Figure 4.7).

All project team members should have a copy of the SOW and refer to it frequently. The SOW is similar to a constitution and should be understood by all those affected by it. Whether analysts, programmers, administrators, or technical writers, everyone should know the goals, objectives, repressibilities, and constraints so they can work accordingly. The SOW should not be treated like a sacred scroll known only to a few. That can only lead to misdirection, misinformation, miscommunication, and misgiving.

The people side of the work breakdown structure

Upon signing the SOW, the project manager can begin planning the project and building a work breakdown structure (WBS).

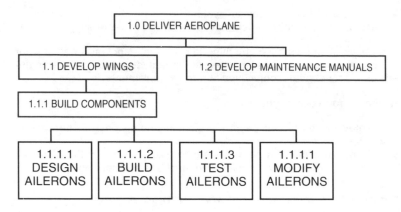

Figure 4.8   *Overview sample of a work breakdown structure*

The WBS is a top-down approach to identifying the tasks and sub-tasks required for developing a product. It starts with a broad subject, such as the name of a product, and explodes it into increasingly finite, measurable tasks and sub-tasks. Once the WBS has been defined to the lowest level, the project manager can use it to estimate times for completing each task or sub-task and constructing a schedule (see Figure 4.8).

Building a work breakdown structure is not mentally taxing but dealing with the people involved makes it a difficult process.

For example, building a useful WBS requires time and plenty of it, but the client may not want to expend that time simply because it would rather devote people to direct line production. Senior management may find the effort costly in the short run because nothing has been produced right away. Team members want to 'produce' rather than do what they consider 'administrivia'.

Not only does building a WBS require time but patience, too. People tend to perceive the task of exploding the WBS differently; that is, the client might tackle it from one perspective, the project manager from another, and team members from still another. Further, there is the review and revisions from senior management. Getting agreement among all those parties can prove burdensome and often requires overcoming

PROJECT MANAGER

- Builds work breakdown structure
- Ensures a realistic work breakdown structure
- Generates meaningful schedules including monitoring and tracking performance
- Monitors and tracks progress
- Transforms work breakdown structure into meaningful schedules, cost estimates, and cost performance

SENIOR MANAGEMENT

- Review the work breakdown structure

CLIENT

- Agrees to the work breakdown structure
- Provides input to work breakdown structure development

PROJECT TEAM

- Assists in building the work breakdown structure
- Agrees to work breakdown structure
- Lists work to be performed
- Tracks progress

Figure 4.9 *Tasks/responsibilities regarding the work breakdown structure*

conflicts (see Figure 4.9). In the end, however, all parties must consent to the WBS before building a schedule – a task that can also try anyone's patience.

Building a WBS also threatens people (see Figure 4.10). They do not want to list the work that they will perform. They may fear being held accountable or constantly being tracked. In other words, they feel that they may lose their autonomy. Many team members, especially those who are prima donnas, feel that way. The client often wants a good WBS so it can track progress, that is, as long as *it* is not being tracked. Senior management will express an interest in a WBS but only at a high level. The project manager prefers a WBS to generate

- Project manager
- Technicians
- Engineers
- Configuration management specialists
- Quality assurance specialists
- Client
- Analysts
- Senior management
- Designers
- Trainers
- Auditors

Figure 4.10   *Some positions providing input to the work break-down structure*

meaningful schedules as well as monitor and track perfor-mance.

Managing the people side of building the WBS

To handle these people side issues which influence the quality of the WBS, you can take several actions. One is to identify who should provide input during the building of the WBS. The degree of input depends on how much the project affects them. The more the project affects them, the more input they should have, and of course, the reverse.

Obtaining their participation offers two advantages. You develop a more comprehensive and useful WBS. It will con-tain more tasks and sub-tasks as well as address more topics. You will also reduce the likelihood of objections and oppo-sitions to your project plans. If people provide input to the WBS, they will be less inclined to criticize your project plans on the grounds that you omitted them or that you imposed tasks upon them.

Another action to take is to have formal sign-offs of the WBS before using it to build schedules. People often will balk at placing their signatures on anything, unless they have confi-dence in what they are signing. Once they sign it, they have committed themselves, and especially so after their commit-ment has been documented. Future criticisms of your WBS should thus subside.

Still another action to take is to place the WBS under strict change control. That action should occur once you have unanimous consent. Placing the WBS in change control prohibits whimsical alterations of the WBS which could affect the validity and reliability of the schedule. Without change control, some team members will claim the schedule (based on the WBS) is no longer accurate and, therefore, no longer relevant.

A final action is to stress continually the importance of the WBS. Emphasize to the client, senior management, and the team that the WBS serves as the basis for making time and cost estimates, building schedules, and tracking time and cost performance. Also ensure that they understand that if the WBS changes, those alterations will affect costs and schedules (for example, the manpower required to complete a task or whether you wish to use automated machinery, such as a mainframe computer).

But estimates play another important role. They enable you to determine which activities are critical and which ones are not. Because you will use estimates to build a schedule, such as a Gantt chart or network diagram (see Figures 4.11 and 4.12), you can determine which tasks are more important than others, known as your critical path.

You can also use estimates to measure performance. If you have reliable estimates (that is, having a high degree of accuracy), you can use them as standards to determine how well project team members have performed. The estimates, in other words, can serve as yardsticks to assess employee performance. Hence, performance evaluation becomes less subjective.

In addition, you can use those estimates to assess how well the project is progressing. With accurate estimates, you track and monitor by noting any variances (the difference between what you planned and what you have actually achieved up to a specific point in time). If you detect a negative variance, you can respond accordingly. Finally, estimates are indispensable for developing a schedule. You must have time estimates to build a schedule (see Figure 4.13).

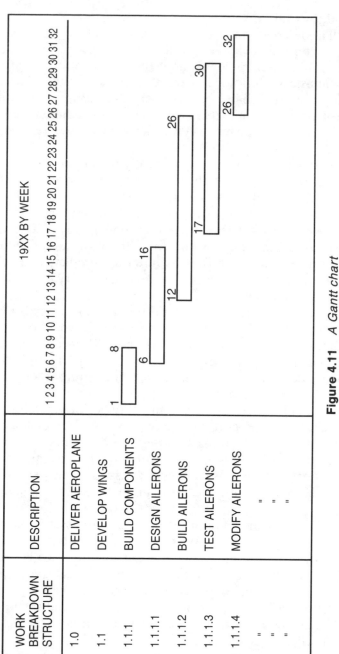

Figure 4.11   *A Gantt chart*

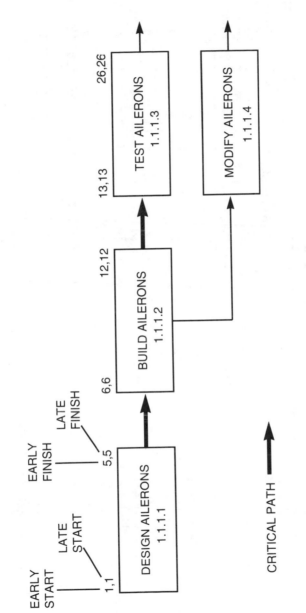

Figure 4.12 *Network diagram*

WORK BREAKDOWN STRUCTURE	DESCRIPTION	ESTIMATE IN HOURS			
		Most Optimistic	Most Pessimistic	Most Likely	Expected*
1.0	Deliver aeroplane				
1.1	Develop wings				
1.1.1	Build components				
1.1.1.1	Design ailerons	6	30	15	16
1.1.1.2	Build ailerons	14	76	51	49
1.1.1.3	Test ailerons	48	96	54	60
1.1.1.4	Modify ailerons	12	80	70	62
....		14	70	51	48

$$*\text{Expected} = \frac{(\text{Most Optimistic}) + 4\,(\text{Most Likely}) + (\text{Most Pessimistic})}{6}$$

Figure 4.15   *Aeroplane system estimate example*

PROJECT MANAGER

> • Compiles time estimates to build a schedule
> • Incorporates time estimates into a schedule

SENIOR MANAGEMENT

> • Provide return on investment guidelines
> • Provide constraints and additional restrictions

CLIENT

> • Provides time estimates
> • Concurs with senior management return on investment guidelines

PROJECT TEAM

> • Provides time estimates for their assignments

Figure 4.14 *Tasks/responsibilities regarding estimating*

The people side of estimating

Estimating requires the participation of many people. That participation is necessary to develop reliable estimates but also raises some interesting people side issues (see Figure 4.14).

Some team members are afraid to make estimates. They may fear reprisal from management for making an inaccurate estimate. They may feel embarrassment if they exceed their estimate, or they may fear overcommitting themselves. When they are forced to make an estimate, their estimates are filled with qualifications that make the estimates meaningless.

Estimating on projects is very difficult because too many unknowns exist (see Figure 4.15 for some of the factors involved). Developing a product depends on a person's previous experience, knowledge, and aptitude. It also depends on the tools and techniques employed as well as the size and complexity of the system being developed. It is not surprising,

- Experience/expertise
- Knowledge
- Aptitude/skills
- Techniques
- Methodologies
- Product size
- Complexity
- Reliability (optimistic to pessimistic estimating parameters)
- Productivity tools
- Contingencies
- Politics
- Quality
- Validity (available information)
- 2nd or 3rd party unbiased opinions
- Timeliness to deliver estimate
- Funding
- Cooperation from internal/external sources
- Communication/Personal relationships
- Fear of not delivering per the estimate
- Distance from core team
- Ill-defined goals, objectives, and requirements
- Warranties

Figure 4.15 *Factors to consider when estimating*

therefore, that some team members are reluctant to commit themselves to a time estimate.

Other people do not hesitate to make an estimate. To them, it is like making a wager. They will gladly give it to you without seriously considering or having any appreciation of the effect of their estimates. These are often meaningless simply because little reasoning went into their formulation. This type of estimating is akin to betting on a horse at the races because the animal has black fur and a white tail. Such estimates are whimsical.

'Super performers' often fall into this trap. They have high expertise in a particular area and often underestimate the time required to complete a task. They assume that they can over-come the complexity of the task with their skills. This over-confidence leads to overlooking factors that they should have considered when developing their initial estimates.

Still other team members inflate estimates. Their motive is sometimes sinister. By inflating the estimate for a task, they can complete it in less time than stated. This is the result they wanted. They look artificially effective and efficient although their performance is the result of a bad estimate and not because they are good performers.

Not all inflated estimates have a sinister motive behind them. Some people give inflated time estimates because they are pessimists. Although appearing harmless, such estimating attitudes can lead to waste. Project managers may allocate more funds than necessary or purchase more supplies than were needed. For instance, they may purchase more hardware or software than is necessary to use on a microcomputer, thereby resulting in thousands of dollars in excess costs.

Some team members deflate their estimates, reflecting extreme optimism. Their positive attitude can translate into problems as soon as a task goes awry. Their estimates do not account for this possibility, thereby causing embarrassment when you report to higher management and the client that you cannot meet an agreed date and may require additional time. It can also cause you to consume scarce time to re-plan.

Some people agree to a bad estimate because someone with higher authority pressured them. Perhaps the boss of a project manager had agreed to a bad estimate because agreement meant good politics with the client. The boss then pressures the project manager to accept the bad estimate. Such estimates may deceive everyone but only for a short time. Once the project begins, the project manager will see and feel the impact of the poor estimate.

Software development projects, for example, have the reputation of being expensive from the perspective of the client. The client wants the product quickly and cheaply with a high level of quality. Senior management want to serve and please the client to maintain ongoing business relationships. This pressure can cause project managers to agree to trim their estimates when they should not have done so.

Project managers also typically face a series of obstacles when acquiring good estimates. Lack of available information is one of the most common. You might need information about a specific task, such as the skills and level of expertise to perform it. Such information is often not readily available. You may need to conduct further research which may require considerable time (which also may not be available). Even if you acquire an estimate, you can face another obstacle. The estimate that you receive may be less than genuine. It could be under- or over-inflated, causing serious distortion in your estimate. Detecting this problem is not easy. There are two ways to overcome it: you can adjust the estimate to compensate, or, you can contact someone else to verify the estimate for accuracy, for example consulting another team member for a second opinion.

Management intervention is another common obstacle to making accurate estimates. Senior management might place pressure on a project manager to take only a specified time to complete one or more tasks, or to derive an estimate too prematurely. In both cases, degradation of reliability and validity of the estimate may occur.

Lack of time is still another obstacle project managers may face. They do not have the time to derive good estimates simply because senior management will not permit it. Consequently, project managers yield to the pressure, mainly due to career interests, and hope that all will work out. If project managers do not express their need for more time, they will face even worse pressures when they concede to unrealistic estimates and do not meet them later in the project.

In addition to lack of time is a dearth of money. Money is not available to supply the resources, such as labour, to develop good estimates. To save money in the short term, project managers reduce time for estimating only to find later that they must request more time because their estimate was not good. The result is embarrassment for the project manager and angry management, or client, or both.

In software development, for example, project managers are under considerable pressure from clients to start 'cutting code'. They know that clients are paying for their projects and demand the most for their money. That means getting the system up and running and not spending laborious hours writing plans. Many project managers yield to the pressure and their own desire to build the system. Later, they often must return to the client to ask for more money and a slide in a schedule.

Many project managers lack cooperation from the client,

their senior management, and their project team. Management may not want to provide time or resources for estimating for political reasons. Or the client will not provide any information. Or team members may not like working on the project and will do anything to hide information that will improve the estimates. Such circumstances can lead to early project failure simply because this lack of cooperation may spread to other aspects of the project.

Quite often, lack of cooperation is due to fear. Team members are reluctant to commit themselves to an estimate for fear of failure. Senior management might fear estimates because they have been 'burned' in the past by estimates and, therefore, would rather have nebulous figures that would not make them accountable to their bosses. The client may fear estimates because they may allocate more time to certain tasks than is necessary and, consequently, pay more.

Closely related to lack of cooperation is lack of communication. Project managers may face insurmountable communication problems that prevent access to important information for making good estimates. Distance often contributes to this obstacle. Team members may be located over a wide area; project managers, therefore, must make estimates on behalf of some members. Clients may not always be accessible, and project managers might have to guess the time required to perform a specific task.

Poor formulation of goals, objectives, and requirements are other obstacles that project managers will sometimes face. Occasionally, people will be assigned as project managers over a venture that has an ill-defined purpose. That makes estimating extremely difficult. If a solid idea of what will result from the project is lacking, then they will be unable to determine exactly how long it will take. Under some circumstances, the objectives and requirements are vague, too, leading to 'guesstimates' rather than estimates.

Poor formulation of goals, objectives and requirements can lead to an inadequate WBS, a proven potent obstacle to good estimating. Without the former, project managers will find it very difficult to determine specifically the time required to perform a given task or the entire project. A cornerstone for a useful work breakdown structure is having well-defined goals, objectives, and requirements. Unless you have that, the WBS will be inadequate, and a useless WBS leads to unreliable estimates.

More often than not, projects begin with everyone having some nebulous notion of what the project will achieve. The client has some vaguer idea about the product and the project manager often has an even vaguer one. This makes estimating difficult because no one has much of an idea what specifically must occur and for how long.

Lack of or poor knowledge of common estimating techniques is another obstacle project managers may face. Frequently, project managers have no idea of the requirements for developing useful estimates. About the only method they know is asking someone for an estimate and using that figure. Or they develop an estimate based upon their own knowledge and experience. More often than not, these estimates are as useful as the scores of the first Soccer World Cup.

Improving the people side of estimating

You *can* improve the people side of estimating. One way is to identify the person who must make an estimate, that is, the person who will do the work. If more than one person will perform the task, hold a joint meeting to develop an estimate that all of them can accept. One scenario is where Jim and Sally are assigned to develop a component of a product. They jointly review and develop an estimate and provide the result to you, the project manager.

Another approach is to have people provide you with an estimate in writing, such as in a memo. You then use the figures and retain the document in your files for protection and verification. Here, Jim and Sally write the estimate in some detail and submit it.

Never take an estimate at face value. If you suspect that a person has deflated or inflated an estimate, seek a second opinion. Then return to the individual who provided the original estimate and negotiate for a more realistic estimate. For example, Tonia (who might be more seasoned than Jim and Sally) can be approached for another viewpoint and perspective. Then, you can re-visit Jim and Sally for modification of their input.

Avoid giving the impression that estimates are 'written in stone'. Communicate that the purpose of estimates is to build a gameplan and serve as a measure for assessing the progress of the project. Do not generate the fear that if they fail to meet the estimate they might as well look for another job. At the same time, do not give the impression that estimates are unimportant. An estimate is just that – an estimate. It is, in its strictest sense, a 50–50 chance of an event occurring. Sometimes, it just does not work out as planned; however, developing that plan (estimate) is 100 per cent necessary.

Whenever changing an estimate, obtain input from all persons affected by the change. That participation will not only help you develop a realistic estimate and assess the total impact of the revision but will also lower resistance. In other words, people will accept a change if they have a say in its development. Any modifications to Jim and Sally's estimate impacts Melissa and Michael's parallel work. Thus, Melissa and Michael must be aware of the change.

Finally, create and retain an 'Estimating' file for reference. Document any lack of cooperation from people who are responsible for providing estimates. You can do that by preparing letters of understanding, memos requesting a response by a certain date or you will assume your estimates are valid, or preparing a document showing the input of not having adequate estimates.

The people side of scheduling

Building schedules, like estimating and work breakdown structures, is not an easy task. What creates them is not the mechanics but the people or people side issues.

Some people resist scheduling because they feel that it infringes upon their professional independence. They see it as a way of treating them as children, keeping track of their work.

Some high performers and other team members feel they are capable of meeting the overall schedule of the project. They do not need to have someone looking over their shoulders tracking and assessing how much has been completed. They might feel that much 'babysitting' from their perspective impedes their performance. In other words, they could concentrate on building the product rather than complying with the schedule.

Others resist scheduling because it smacks of a police state mentality. They see it as management tracing every move, waiting for the moment to discipline the employee for the slightest infraction, such as missing a completion date.

Still others fight scheduling because they feel it inhibits creativity. They claim that working to a timetable makes employees feel rushed and that, consequently, such an environment represses the urge to create. Ironically, scheduling techniques had their origins in research and development environments, places which require creativity.

Finally, some people resist scheduling because it involves nothing more than additional administrative hassles. Building sound schedules, instituting solid tracking, and providing good monitoring are nothing more than measures for interfering with people doing the real work.

Under rare circumstances these objections may have some credence; in general, they have little validity. Scheduling does not inhibit creativity, it directs it. Creative writers do not just put sentences together haphazardly to create an essay; they follow the rules of the language and organization to produce a work that is comprehensible.

Nor does scheduling reflect a police state mentality. If senior management or the project manager uses schedules as a weapon then the fault lies with them, not with scheduling. A schedule is a tool, just like management by objectives (MBO) and quality control, to manage and not regulate work performance. Its abuse, like other methods of assessment and evaluation, depends on who is using it.

Nor is scheduling an administrative nuisance. Management needs it to have some reasonable assurance that people know how to reach their destination and to keep track of how well they are proceeding towards it. Quite often, people who see scheduling an annoyance are fearful that it may disclose something unsatisfactory about their performance.

- Project manager
- Senior management
- Client
- Supervisors
- Technicians
- Engineers
- Configuration management specialists
- Quality assurance specialists
- Analysts
- Writers
- Lawyers
- Auditors
- Designers
- Trainers

Figure 4.16 *Some of the parties providing input to the schedule*

Managing the people side of scheduling

To make the people side of scheduling easier, you can take some precautionary steps.

Never put a draft schedule in final form. It psychologically affects the quality of feedback you receive from people. They are reluctant to criticize something that appears in final form. They feel that you have done considerable work – and you may have – to build the schedule. If senior management, the client, or team members see something incorrect, they may feel that changing it may require considerable effort and may hurt your feelings. Keep the schedule in draft form until it has received complete approval.

Use both individual sessions and group meetings to build the schedule. You do not have to build the schedule yourself. Indeed, that may very well prove a mistake later in the project, you could face objections from someone later on. The idea is to create a schedule that everyone accepts, that is, one they agree to follow.

The best approach is to determine who should participate in building the schedule (see Figure 4.16 for a sample list). You will probably have identified all those individuals after creating the WBS. You should sit with each person, individually at first, and draft that portion of the schedule pertaining to them. Having received feedback from members of the client and project team, you then hold a group meeting(s). At the meeting, you resolve disagreements until the schedule is acceptable to everyone.

After achieving consensus, obtain everyone's signature on the schedule. Record the date of signing, too. This action signifies agreement to work to the schedule.

Obtaining signatures is more than receiving approval, although that is important. It also has a psychological impact. When someone signs a document, they commit themselves and that commitment is recorded. It then becomes very difficult for them to renege on that commitment without embarrassment and subsequent ramifications.

Armed with signatures from everyone, you place the schedule in final form. Store the original in a safe place and give copies to each of the people on the project and other interested parties. The worse action that you can take is to develop a schedule and hide it. Make sure everyone who needs a schedule has one.

Because you now have the schedule in final form does not mean you cannot change it periodically. Occasionally, you may have to reschedule, and you should archive previous versions of the schedule when this occurs. This action provides excellent traceability on what caused the rescheduling to occur. It also provides powerful information for future projects of a similar nature.

Senior management and the client often appreciate schedules. The former can allocate the monies and long-range plans. The latter feels comfortable with a schedule, knowing that they can expect their product by a certain date. Scheduling, therefore, makes good sense to these two parties. The problem is that some team members dislike scheduling because they are the ones who commit themselves.

The people side sets the stage

The people side of project management plays a critical role in the beginning of a project. It sets the stage for how well the project has been handled in subsequent phases. If all parties cooperate and communicate with one another during planning then managing according to those plans will become somewhat easier. However, if little or no cooperation and communication exists between some or all parties at the start that discord will recur later in the project.

Chapter 5

The people side of budgeting

The allocation of money in a project, often referred to as budgeting, involves more than cash. It entails a complex interplay between the client, project team, project manager, and senior management (see Figure 5.1 for the roles of those four). All four parties must agree to the amounts allocated to each activity in the project and for the entire project. Because money is often available in limited quantities all parties must negotiate with one another, and that process can generate a wide range of people side issues.

An overview of the budgeting process

The process of allocating money has a tremendous impact on the people side of project management. This is because it involves competition, negotiation, and politics that determine who gets what and when.

The budgeting process usually works this way. The client wants a product built that has certain features and capabilities. Senior management want to accommodate the request to generate revenue to sustain operations and work in new areas. The project manager needs as much money as possible to complete the project based upon estimates from the project team.

All three parties then negotiate among themselves the

amount of money to complete the project. The process (see Figure 5.2) involves a feasibility study to determine if the project is possible and cost-effective. Then, all three parties negotiate a statement of work that specifies the amount of money that will be available for completing the project.

PROJECT MANAGER

- Ensures that project team completes its tasks
- Orchestrates the project cost-effectively
- Satisfies needs of senior management to keep client satisfied
- Provides opportunities for future business
- Requests additional funding if required
- Tracks and monitors progress regarding expenditures
- Minimizes satisficing (willingness to settle for less)

SENIOR MANAGEMENT

- Maintain open communications with client
- Keep development funding flowing
- Maintain satisfactory client relationship
- Increase opportunity to develop additional projects
- Provide political astuteness
- Balance need for autonomy versus funding pressures

CLIENT

- Generates project request containing rough estimate of funding required
- Allocates/re-allocates funding based upon progress and money expended
- Re-evaluates priorities regarding expenditures
- Modifies system requirements versus available funding
- Assesses risk versus payoff

PROJECT TEAM

- Builds the system efficiently and effectively
- Communicates to project manager anticipated circumstances requiring additional funding

Figure 5.1 *Tasks/responsibilities regarding the budget*

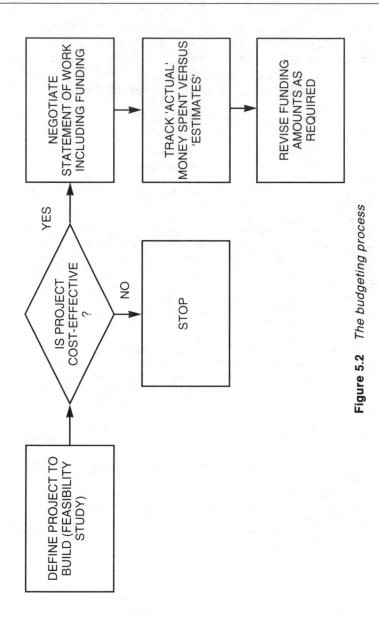

Figure 5.2 *The budgeting process*

As the project proceeds, all parties track the amount actually spent up to a given point in time (known as actuals), to that which should have been spent (the estimates). All parties will also maintain the amount of projected expenditure for completing each task and the entire project, known as estimate-at-completion.

Ideally, all actuals should match the estimates, from the start to the end of the project. Frequently, however, no match exists. That causes several issues to arise concerning the people side of project management, because the client, project manager, senior management, and the project team operate from different perspectives.

The client perspective

The client brings its own perspective to the budgeting process. Often, this conflicts with the project manager, the project team, and senior management.

First, the client pays the bills and it knows it. It recognizes that the project would not exist if it had not generated the request. Being the sole or primary source of revenue, it expects top performance at minimum cost. This attitude can place severe pressure on senior management, the project manager, and the project team to perform accordingly.

Second, the client often wants more for less. That is, it expects the project manager and the project team to produce at a rapid but effective pace. This, too, can place severe pressure on senior management, the project manager, and the project team.

Finally, the client expects immediate feedback for its money. Using techniques that do not provide immediate feedback can frustrate the user who fails to understand the true lag time required to define requirements and produce output. The client starts to wonder what it is paying for.

These perspectives have their merit. The client should expect its money to be well spent for the product it will receive. Taken to an extreme, however, such a perspective during the budget process could prove hazardous. The client could use money as a weapon by threatening to curtail, reduce, or reallocate funds. Taking this one step further, it could reduce the independence of the project manager and project team.

The senior management perspective

Senior management have their own perspective that they bring to the budgeting process too, and this can lead to conflict.

First, senior management seek to maintain an ongoing relationship with the client. In other words they want the money. Without that money, activities would become marginal.

Second, senior management want a satisfied client. If satisfied, the client will continue the existing project and start others. That results in sustained employment and a highly competent staff.

Third, they do not want the client to take advantage of them. That is, they want to provide the necessary support for projects but not by absorbing any of the costs themselves. Hence, they can find themselves on a tightrope, balancing the need for obtaining funds for a project but not pushing too hard for fear of losing the funding.

Quite often, the senior management perspective can create problems. Senior management can become cautious and conservative in their approach towards managing a project. Indeed, they might even appear indecisive. Taking their perspective to the extreme, senior management can become an obstacle to progress by blocking communications, micromanaging the project, and generating political conflict.

The project team perspective

Like the client and senior management, the project team has its own perspective which can influence how well the budget process is handled.

The project team wants to go to work right away, that is, to build the product. But they can only do that if they have the money available. That requires obtaining sufficient funds to start the project with the right tools, and that is when people side issues start to emerge.

Often, the team wants the state-of-the-art tools to build the product. If those tools are not already available, the client often must pay for them.

The client, wanting the most for the least money, resists fulfilling requests with a blank cheque. It wants to keep the budget down and not pay for equipment destined for some other future project. The project manager must somehow reconcile these different desires so that costs are contained and the team can perform effectively.

The project team often has another interest. It seeks enough money for contingencies as well as for performing expected tasks. While the project budget should account for unexpected events, this amount is often less than desired and quite often disappears early in a project. Consequently, the client seeks to minimize additional expenditures by resisting the allocation of additional funds. It often places pressure on the project manager to cut costs from the existing budget to lessen the chance of an overrun. Team members begin to feel that they are working to satisfy the 'bean counters' rather than to build a product. In other words, they are concentrating on efficiency rather than effectiveness for fear of a budget overrun. The project manager once again must reconcile the need to curtail costs (that is, satisfy the client) and complete the project according to acceptable professional standards.

The project manager's perspective

Project managers must manage the budgetary affairs of their project as though walking a tightrope. They must ensure that the project team completes its tasks while at the same time doing so within a limited budget. They must also satisfy the needs of their senior management, that is, keep the client happy and keep opportunities open for future business.

Project managers, therefore, play a central role in the people side of budgeting. Here are some actions that you can take to ensure that the people side of budgeting is as smooth as possible for you.

Different perspectives

Recognize that several perspectives exist in the budgeting process. Project managers must avoid the tendency to see budgetary matters from one perspective only. They might view budgetary issues from a technical perspective which could mean siding with the project team. They might yield to the pressure of senior management by committing themselves to unrealistic or inadequate budgets.

You must not, therefore, subscribe to a myopic viewpoint. That could lead to taking sides which can build communication walls between yourself and other project participants. That, in turn, can cause problems when handling the people side of budgeting.

Realistic expectations

A tendency exists for projects to start on a natural high, which everyone is excited to get started. The client wants to have the product as soon as possible; senior management want it to serve as a vehicle for future work; project team members want to use their skills and expand their experience; and the project manager wants to manage the project cost-effectively.

This enthusiasm soon clashes with the reality of not only having limited time but also limited budgets. This confrontation is hard if people possess unrealistic expectations. Disillusionment can result as all participants struggle for control over limited funds. The project, as regards budgetary matters, becomes a tragedy of the commons where everyone fights one another for limited funds.

Cost-cutting

Some project managers react to a possible budget overrun by slashing costs across the board. They might, for instance, receive pressure from the client or senior management to cut costs by ten per cent, and they respond by reducing all expenditures by that amount.

Such action has dire consequences. They may cut costs on critical activities or purchases that will improve matters in the short run but lead to worse circumstances in the long run. This strait-jacket approach to cost-cutting will have serious effects not only on expenditures but on the project team too.

Team members will feel pressure to perform with less which, in turn, can affect their attitude, morale, and performance. For example, they might have to work using substandard tools. Later, their productivity may decline and budget overruns occur due to having to hire additional staff, have people work overtime, or purchase more tools. The ten per cent cut earlier becomes a much costlier budget increase later in the project.

If you must reduce costs, you should avoid the cost-cutting approach unless absolutely necessary. Explore alternative means, such as streamlining administrative activities and reduce costs only in those areas that do not seriously affect the progress of the project. That way you will lessen the impact on the productivity of team members and pressure from senior management and the client.

Predictive budgeting

One of the quickest ways to raise people side problems is to present the client and senior management with a request for additional funding without prior warning. In this situation, project managers cannot help but appear not in control of their projects.

The best way to prevent taking the client or senior management by surprise is to use predictive budgeting. In this way project managers not only keep track of what has been spent but what will be spent if the current pace and mode of operation continue. Project managers, therefore, must not only track costs but monitor them. That arms them with the capability to inform senior management and the client of any possible future requests for additional resources. Senior management and the client can then prepare for the possibility of allocating more money.

Honesty

Although trite, 'honesty is the best policy' in budgeting. If programme managers need more money, they should state the case and the reasons for their requests. Attempting to outwit the client by using exotic budgeting techniques to conceal expenditure will only encourage suspicions between all parties. Any such measures for concealing costs will hinder the people side management of projects.

If you face a budgetary problem you should document the reasons for the increase. That might entail reviewing project history files, compiling statistics, and developing alternative plans. Then you should state your case to senior management and the client using your findings. Never go to the client or senior management simply requesting or downplaying the request for additional funds. That will only increase suspicions and make managing the people side of budgeting a more difficult task.

Joint participation

The people side of budgeting involves more sensitivity than any of the other functions dealing with managing projects. Money is the source from which all actions start; without money and the desire for it no projects would exist. Everyone – the client, senior management, project team, and the project manager – must manage this resource efficiently and effectively. If not managed well, managing the people side of budgeting can prove difficult.

If you invite everyone into the budgeting process (that is, obtain input, feedback, and consensus) all parties will hesitate before pinpointing blame, hoarding cash reserves, or deliberately miscommunicating, and these will be less even if a budget overrun occurs. Everyone will better understand the reasons for the original budget and the circumstances leading to a budget overrun.

Hardside is people side

The hardside of the budgetary process entails more than calculating costs using software or a calculator. It involves the sensitivities of many people. Unless these are considered, the budgetary process can affect the outcome and, consequently, the performance of the project.

Chapter 6

The people side of change management

Change in projects is inescapable. Changes originate from the client, team, senior management, and the market. They can deal with any aspect of the project life cycle and can cause changes to project management practices, including scheduling, estimating, and budgeting (see Figure 6.1). Instituting such changes upsets the status quo and can have a profound affect on productivity unless managed well.

What change management is

Change management aims to alter the status quo in a manner that minimizes negative effects on productivity. Achieving that aim is not easy since people are involved.

The secret to change management is to prepare people for change which means not giving them surprises or catching them off guard. If you fail to prepare them, you will meet resistance. Turnover and absenteeism are just two ways people express their disapproval of change. Other ways include sabotaging change (such as not complying with it) and finding alternatives to change (like doing the work manually rather than using a computer).

- Statement of work
- Work breakdown structure
- Requirements
- Specifications
- Design
- Product
- Communication media
- Documentation (electronic and hardcopy)
- Text and graphics (Narrative with accompanying pictures)
- Drawings
- Internal and external interfaces
- Processes
- Methodologies/techniques
- Schedules
- Estimates
- Budgets
- Hardware
- Software
- Staff/organization
- Vendor offerings

Figure 6.1 *Typical project change areas*

Ways to manage change

Several ways exist for you to prepare people for change.

Strive to acquire the participation of everyone who will be affected by change. If you change the work breakdown structure or requirements definition, for example, determine who will be impacted by the change and solicit their feedback. Also, obtain their signature on all relevant documentation to record their approval. You should repeat these actions for all important documentation. By acquiring their participation, you effectively negate any potential opposition. An example is of engineers on an aerospace project designing the body of a commuter plane. The client determined that a shift in the market required considerable revision of the design. Feedback from the engineers, among others, will be required to determine the impact of this change. Formal change procedures would then be undertaken and approved with date and signature blocks.

Strive for open communications up and down the chain of

1. Identify requested change on paper for change control approval*
2. Requested change must be signed off by requester and their immediate supervisor
3. Change approval team evaluates requests and determines whether
   approved, rejected, or deferred
4. If approved, the requested change is scheduled for work
5. If rejected, the requested change is shelved
6. If deferred, the requested change is either placed on hold or re-written
   and resubmitted for evaluation

NOTE: All requested changes and their dispositions are documented and
kept as a permanent record (e.g., placed in a ring binder)

*Establish change control approval team consisting of project manager,
team members, and secretary (for taking minutes)

Figure 6.2   *Typical change control function*

command and laterally with the user. Be frank with all parties
about any changes. The minute suspicions arise over your
motives and credibility, you will receive little support for your
new plans. Address the change(s) straight. If you feel they are
large say so. If, for example, the client feels otherwise, still
express your opinion. This creates the opportunity for discussion and saves potential problems in the long run.

In addition, prepare everyone for the new plans. Avoid
surprises to preclude resistance. Hold mini-training sessions
about the new plans, highlighting what has and has not
changed and why. Give people new documentation to use. Let
them know whom to contact for questions (and answers).
Remove as many obstacles to the change before it takes effect.
That will make your job easier. In summary, prepare prior to
implementing a change. By informing them that a change is
coming, you can stimulate pre-planning on how to incorporate it (see Figure 6.2).

You must sell the change too. People will accept change if
they realize its benefits and the problems or costs involved in
maintaining the status quo. Effective selling makes people

think they need the change. That requires explaining to project participants, from their perspective, why a change is necessary. You should avoid giving the impression that the change will mean instant improvement and will go smoothly. That may occur but more often it does not. You should mention that difficulties will arise and provide suggestions for overcoming them. Making a change in the specifications, for example, can improve the system's performance, but it might take time. Sometimes the 'answer' gives rise to further questions.

As a project manager, you need patience to deal with change because handling its dynamics is strenuous. Not everything will go according to your new plan; indeed, your new plans may occasionally need revisions. You need to psychologically adapt to such environments to handle the stress that accompanies change. Technical projects involve working in a flexible environment. For example, technology used in data processing projects can quickly become outmoded. New hardware and software entering the marketplace may necessitate re-evaluating existing tools and replacing some or all of them. This transition often is not easy and may require going back to stage one. Thus, the project manager needs to retain emotional balance.

Occasionally, some project participants resist change for the sake of it. They will do anything to obstruct change. Using peer pressure can often turn the most stalwart resister around. If others support the change, have them sell for you. Let them pressure your opposition to support your changes. If opposition continues, do what most people do when facing a brick wall; either go around it or tear it down. The ideal is to obtain people's support for a change, if possible, by making them think they requested it.

You must also recognize that change requires three parties participating: your team, your management, and the client. Without their support, you will find implementing change very difficult. If changing the schedule without the client's concurrence, for example, you will lack cooperation and may possibly face litigation. If you fail to consult with your project team, you may find that certain members will feel like pawns and alienated. Consequently, they will reduce their level of performance. If you failed to consult with senior management, they may feel slighted and may respond by decreasing future political and financial support.

A change may make good rational, technical sense, but often that is not enough for effective implementation. You must recognize effective change management involves playing politics and you have three participants to deal with.

The change target is the first. It may be a person, place, organization, thing, or group of people. It is the object of the change. A change target could be the client or the project team. In some instances, it could be senior management. These change targets will respond to change in varying degrees.

The change sponsor is the second. This may be a person, group of people, or organization. It provides the political muscle to effect a change. That could mean providing the necessary resources to announce its support to the organization. Typically, change sponsors come from senior management.

The change agent is the third. It may be either a person, group, or organization. It actually plans, organizes, and executes a change. It works as a catalyst for a change. Change agents are usually project managers because of their unique position.

The reality of change is that it cannot be avoided. Some changes make good sense while others do not, but project managers must know how to introduce such changes to ensure that relations with the client, senior management, and the team sustain productivity so that the project completes on time, within budget, and to the highest workmanship.

Chapter 7

Knowing what is going on

Project managers must follow their plans. Little sense exists in investing much time and money in building plans and then never taking time to ensure that everyone (including themselves) follows them.

Yet not only do few project managers plan but they very rarely follow the plans they have developed. They may build an elaborate plan perhaps to prove to their management and themselves that they know what they are doing. Then they quickly deviate from it.

The result is project managers with a reactive style of management. The project is replete with examples of management by confusion, management by drives, and management by crisis. Project managers soon ask themselves: What went wrong?

Detecting variances to plans

As a project manager, you must establish measures that help you to detect deviations from your plans. Before implementing those measures, however, you must remember the following points.

Always be vigilant about detecting variances to your plans. A variance is the difference between what you had planned and what has actually occurred at any point in time. A variance typically relates to budget and schedule items. Variance detection requires the project manager to acquire expertise in exception reporting.

Variances are classified as either positive, negative, or neutral. For a schedule, a positive variance occurs when a milestone, or event, actually starts or finishes before what was planned. Conversely, a negative variance is one when a milestone, or event, actually starts or finishes after what was planned. For a budget, a positive variance is an underrun when a project spends less than expected. Conversely, a negative variance is an overrun where a project spends more than anticipated. A neutral variance is when no difference exists between planned and actual circumstances.

Of course, an underrun in the budget or ahead of schedule condition does not necessarily signify a favourable situation. Sometimes, a positive variance can mean negative circumstances. For example, an ahead of schedule condition may indicate that the project team is sacrificing quality. Also, a positive variance in the budget may mean that the team's workmanship is unsatisfactory.

As a project manager, you must always concern yourself with the validity of your information. Perhaps the information is tainted. For instance, someone says a task is 100 per cent complete. Should you believe that report?

Or perhaps you are not receiving information but data. Data are not meaningful; data are merely the compilation of facts and figures. Information is facts and figures that you find meaningful; that is, you find it useful.

In today's computing environment, many project managers receive data, not information, and they receive more than they need. Somehow, they must pick from the pile what they find useful, which is not easy.

Having data rather than information is not the only threat to validity. Project managers may receive information that is a downright lie. For example, some people may say their mark is 100 per cent complete when it is not. They lied to avoid looking bad or to remove pressure on them.

Some people will massage information to avoid alarming

you when you should really feel alarmed. They may say something like, 'Yes, we are exceeding the budget. But that is only temporary as far as I can tell.'

Other people will mimic information back to you. They can read on your face what you want to hear, and they are only too glad to comply. In other words, they tell you what you want to hear and not what you need to hear.

You can also receive slanted information. You may only receive one perspective when many viewpoints are necessary. This exists when seeking assessments based upon opinions rather than hard facts.

But project managers can even slant the information themselves. They will simply ignore certain information that they receive, particularly when negative. They may not want to hear that they will miss the project completion date, or they may incorrectly interpret information. In other words, they hear only what they want to hear.

In addition, you may receive incomplete information. You fail to receive all the facts. For example, you receive budget information but not any related to the schedule or quality. Lacking the other information hinders sound assessments and decisions.

Obtaining complete, accurate information in software development is a difficult, demanding task. That is because building a system requires many unknown factors that one does not face on, for example, construction projects. Too many ifs and unpredictable factors militate against receiving good, useful information. Software development projects contain a high degree of intangibility. Telling Santa while sitting on his knee that you want an electric train is very different from telling the software development folks that for a proposed light rail mass transit system you need some software to 'run the thing'.

Both sets of requirements are wish lists. However, the reality of Santa's electric train can take many forms almost all of which will delight the young requestor. On the other hand, software deliverables for a mass transit system are fraught with challenges and opportunities. Expecting the unexpected may be standard trade jargon, but getting what you ask for is yet another matter.

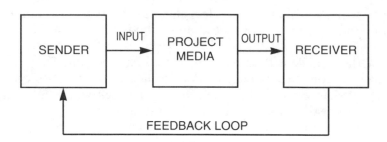

Figure 7.1   *Project information flow*

The communication system

Problems with validity result from a failure in the feedback loop that exists for every project. In every project, senders and receivers participate in a communication system. The senders may be your client, management, or team; the receivers may be the same people. Information passes between the senders and receivers, as shown in Figure 7.1. The sender passes information to the receiver using project media (such as memos and telephones). The receiver then responds to the information or messages. The response is in the form of information. This ping-pong effect with information is known as feedback, and flows through a loop.

Occasionally, the feedback loop collapses. Information becomes distorted and loses its validity. Project managers must learn to become sceptics to detect when corruption of the information occurs. That means constantly asking themselves whether the information they receive is valid.

No project is perfect. Inevitably, the communication process on a project will fail. As long as people work on a project, they will distort information. Project managers must remind themselves of this if they want a clear picture about the status of their projects.

Always remember also that a distinction exists between tracking and monitoring. Tracking requires looking at the past. It is based upon the assumption that by knowing the past you can understand the present. You can also tell whether performance was satisfactory. Tracking, therefore, allows you to discern what went well and what did not.

Monitoring requires looking into the future. You need to assess where you will finish if previous circumstances continue. The future is based upon the past and the present. Monitoring, enables you to take positive action now so the project proceeds well in the future.

Hence, you must know where you have been, where you are, and where you will be. One of your main tools to accomplish that is the meeting.

Using meetings to collect data

Most people have attended meetings in their working careers, some good and some bad. Good meetings are those that are productive. They contribute to effective communications, lead to greater productivity, build team spirit, increase individual morale, and reduce misinterpretations. Bad meetings contribute little or none of those items.

As a project manager, you have to manage your time effectively for your project. You will therefore want to conduct and spend your time in good meetings. If you want productive meetings, consider the following guidelines.

Whenever you hold a meeting, create an agenda. List the major topics, by importance, on a sheet. It is good practice to indicate the length of time for discussion of each topic. You then send the agenda to the attendees.

An agenda serves several purposes. It lets everyone know in advance the topics you will cover in the meeting. It also acts as a control mechanism to prevent the meeting from going astray, such as by discussing superfluous topics.

Schedule a time and place agreeable to everyone attending. That requires considerable coordination but coordination is the job of the project manager. Factors such the calendar day and the clock time and determining whether to hold the meetings onsite or offsite must be decided.

Onsite meetings offer many benefits. Everyone can conveniently attend because the place is centrally located. The services and equipment to conduct the meetings are readily available.

Holding meetings onsite, however has its problems. People

are frequently pulled out from the meeting. Someone can interrupt it for what that person considers a more important matter.

Offsite meetings offer some benefits that overcome the difficulties related to onsite meetings. You do not have interruptions or lose people. There are problems however. Offsite meetings are expensive and difficult to coordinate. Also, people must make an extra effort to find the location. It may not be conveniently located.

As a project manager, most of your meetings are onsite. That means you must be extra careful to minimize opportunities for interruptions and people being pulled away.

You can do that by holding regularly scheduled meetings, requesting everyone to remain for the entire duration, and stressing the importance of their participation.

Furthermore, identify clearly who must attend which meetings. That will ensure the right people at the right meeting. Some people, including the client, may not belong at a specific meeting. Perhaps certain team members should not attend. The responsibility rests with you, the project manager, to let people know who are and who are not to attend specific meetings.

Above all, avoid having an unusually large number of people at a meeting. Ten is about the maximum number. More than ten can lead to factioning that hinders consensus. Remember, project managers build consensus, not hold plenary sessions.

Upon scheduling a meeting, distribute a memo to all attendees. Inform, or remind, them of the time, place, and subject. Keep the memo brief. Attach any supplementary material that they should review prior to the meeting. Remind them in the memo that they should do so and bring the material with them.

Never allow a meeting to continue endlessly. If the meeting is lengthy, hold periodic breaks so people remain alert. Breaks allow people to refresh themselves for the next hour.

If the meeting is to last several hours, for example three or more, consider breaking it into sessions. People can take in only so much information, and they will grow restless regardless of the breaks that you give them. You can either schedule several sessions in advance, or you can acquire consensus when the next session occurs.

Also consider the time of day to hold a meeting. Holding a meeting half-an-hour before lunchtime or closing time may not lead to productive results. Some project managers have even held meetings at 4 pm on a Friday afternoon. Selecting such ludicrous times creates unhappiness rather than greater productivity.

As a project manager, you must engender the right atmosphere at meetings. You want a 'win–win' rather than a 'win–lose' environment. If it has an atmosphere of winners and losers, then the meeting will fail. Team spirit will decline; communication will collapse; and, everyone will go in separate directions. Ultimately, productivity declines, which translates into schedule slides, budget overruns, and quality degradation.

When running meetings, you are the chairperson. That does not mean dominating the meeting. Nor does it mean suppressing any disagreements. It does mean ensuring the meeting progresses by encouraging communications, problem-solving, and team unity. The responsibility for a successful meeting rests with you.

Types of meetings

As a project manager, you will hold several types of meetings. These can be divided into regular and ad hoc meetings.

Regular meetings occur at specific intervals, e.g., on the first Monday of every month or at the end of a major phase or development of a sub-product.

One regular meeting is the checkpoint review meeting. These meetings occur whenever a specific milestone occurs, such as completing a sub-product or a phase. Attendees include the project manager, customer representatives, and senior management. They discuss major issues that have arisen and determine whether to proceed, repeat work, or even to terminate the project.

Below is a typical agenda for a checkpoint review meeting:

- Successes
- Problems
- Remaining issues
- Actions and responsibilities to resolve issues
- Decision whether to proceed

Another regular meeting is the status review meeting. These meetings occur at specific intervals, such as weekly or bi-weekly. The purpose is to acquire information on the project's progress regarding schedule, budget, and quality. Attendees include the project manager, team leaders, and customer representatives. After acquiring the appropriate information, you can assess how well the project has progressed.

Project managers can have a tremendous impact on the productivity of a status review meeting. If the project manager does all the talking and asks few questions, feedback becomes minimal and can lead to poor decision-making.

They can also inhibit feedback in another way. Rather than waiting for feedback from each attendee, they criticize the person giving the first negative feedback. Their criticism then inhibits meaningful feedback from the other attendees for fear of embarrassment. The result is only the information that the project managers want to, not need to, hear.

Below is a typical agenda for a status review meeting:

- Announcements
- Feedback from each attendee regarding schedule, budget, and quality
- Discussion of successes
- Discussion of problems
- Possible solutions to problems
- Open discussion

Staff meetings are the third type of regularly scheduled meeting. These are meetings usually held once a week where only team members attend; neither the customer or senior management is present. These meetings typically last no more than an hour and cover several topics. Team members discuss successes and failures and disseminate important information to each other. This meeting should have a win–win atmosphere to preclude inhibiting discussion.

The meeting, however, is not a stage for project managers to pontificate for two hours. Instead, they must use the meeting to encourage communication up and down the chain of command. Project managers can also use the meeting to build esprit de corps and facilitate problem-solving. Below is a typical agenda for staff meetings:

- Announcements by the project manager
- Discussion of significant issues affecting progress
- Announcements, questions, and comments by each team member

Not only do you have regularly scheduled meetings, but also ad hoc ones. These are meetings occurring whenever the need arises. The two principal types of ad hoc meetings are quality reviews and individual sessions.

Quality reviews are held to assess the level of workmanship for a component of a product. Certain team members, the client, and the project manager attend to ensure that the work has been done satisfactorily and that the output meets requirements according to company standards.

The number of attendees is small, no more than ten people. Someone serves as the referee to ensure that no one dominates the session, or everyone sways from the topic; or, that it degenerates into a debating society. Another person takes minutes to ensure everyone complies with their commitments and to record the results of the session. He or she also obtains signatures on the minutes and distributes a copy to all participants.

An open atmosphere is absolutely essential to allow the free exchange of ideas and permit a rigorous evaluation of the output. After the meeting, everyone shares responsibility for the outcome, especially if the group approves the output.

Although project managers participate in quality reviews, they do not plan, organize, and conduct them. That work is done by the presenter or another team member. You are responsible for ensuring that quality reviews occur and in a manner that increases productivity.

Below is a typical agenda for a quality review meeting:

- Introduction of the topic

- Responsibilities during the session
- What the session should achieve
- Group verdict
- Whether another session is necessary

Another ad hoc meeting is the short session held periodically with each team member by the project manager. During the session, they discuss the current and future tasks of the team member and some of the successes and obstacles they have faced or will face. These sessions are held in the strictest confidence. If the project managers violate that confidence in any way, the relationship between the team member and the project manager will deteriorate.

Although not a meeting per se, Management By Walking Around (MBWA) is another way to acquire feedback about your project. The idea is to circulate among project participants to keep abreast of activities in your environment. That does not mean doing the work for them or eliminating their autonomy or ignoring the chain of command. It does mean becoming more aware by moving about and talking with your people. It keeps you up-to-date on major issues.

Effective yet...

Meetings are an effective tool for acquiring an accurate assessment of the project. Yet, as with any other communication medium, you should remain sceptical about the information that you receive. It may be tainted. Extreme pressure to conform, known as group think, can distort the quality of the information. The tendency towards conformity at meetings can give project managers a very misleading impression.

Chapter 8

The political jungle

Although many project managers consider 'politics' a dirty word, they encounter it daily. They can never escape its presence, and the project managers who try to avoid it will fail to manage their projects successfully (see Figure 8.1).

What is 'politics'?

Politics really means the power struggle where people compete with one another to have their say and way. They may compete for more money, to acquire resources, or to bargain with

- Political suicide (losing your job), not political survival
- Limited or no opportunity for influence and decision-making
- Limited or no opportunity for power and control
- Reduced quantity and/or quality of resources (e.g. manpower, funding, equipment, software)
- Lack of 'successful' or 'significant' connotation attached to you and the projects you are assigned
- Ammunition for your enemies
- Limited or no visibility to upper management
- Limited or no opportunity for mentor or sponsor support
- Someone else's scapegoat

Figure 8.1 *Consequences of not being aware of politics*

management and other project managers. And the goal is to satisfy wants, not necessarily needs.

Politics especially manifests itself in a project environment. Employees work for project managers who lack the power to give raises or administer discipline. The project managers compete for scarce resources, such as money, equipment, and people, over which they have little control.

But politics appears in all aspects of business, whether in management or among the rank-and-file. Politics is a reality; all environments are political in one way or another.

The client wants a product at the lowest possible price and effort but of the highest quality. The team members seek to apply their expertise in a cost-effective and qualitative manner. The project manager wants to build the product on schedule, within budget, and of superior quality. All parties are striving for the same goal, that is, to deliver a product. The issue is often over whose 'agenda' determines the direction and modus operandi of the project.

The key to survival as a project manager in a political environment means employing tactics that to some project managers may not appear professional. If you subscribe to that school of thought, you can ignore this chapter but at your own peril. If you want to survive – not necessarily being the victor – this chapter should interest you. Incidentally, you can still be professional and survive politically.

Discovering the political environment

Before you can perform in a highly political environment, you must assess the atmosphere. That means looking at more than the physical environment, acquiring as much information as possible about the non-tangible factors. In fact, the physical environment frequently reveals the non-tangible factors which give you information about your political environment.

Role perceptions are one indicator. Your management has certain perceptions concerning the behaviour or performance of a project manager. The customer has certain perceptions, as does your project team. These perceptions raise expectations about what project managers must do and how they should behave.

You can experience serious problems if you contradict these perceptions. For instance, your management may expect you to have a very dominating influence over the affairs of your project if it places little value on participative management. But your style is very participative. As a result, management may view your style as a weakness.

They may, for example, regard certain individuals on your team as prima donnas whose place is to work and not participate in meetings with the client. Yet these individuals might be attending the meetings to acquire or clarify requirements. You receive pressure from both parties and yield to the team members because the project benefits in the long run. This circumstance occurs frequently and leads to tension because many team members make comments that show a lack of appreciation of the business perspective of the project and thereby raise a political storm.

You may occasionally face conflicting expectations concerning a project manager's role. Again, management might expect you to adopt an authoritarian style. Yet, your team seeks a participative management style. Conflict will arise that can make project management very difficult. Even your own perceptions of a project manager's role may conflict with management, the team, and the client.

Another clue to the political environment is the values that an organization hold supreme. These values, some officially promulgated and others not, are often sanctified by management and employees alike. Violating these values can have severe repercussions, include dismissal.

These values, consisting of norms and beliefs, are expressed in several ways. Company newsletters, policies, and procedures are three ways values are communicated to the workforce and to others. You can also learn the value system in less formal ways, e.g. conversing with employees.

Learning the informal power structure is another way to ascertain an organization's political environment. All organizations have a formal chain of command that is reflected in an organization chart. On paper, it reveals the formal power relationships between individuals. Sometimes, however, the charts fail to reveal the real locus of power. The informal structure, that is the one not reflected in the published organization chart, usually has much more power.

On some projects, a project manager may officially lead a project. Informally, however, another individual – by virtue of their knowledge, expertise, experience, personality, or contacts – will have greater influence over the direction of the project.

Still, do not discount the importance of the formal organization chart. One chart by itself means very little, but looking at several charts issued over a period of time can reveal something about the political environment. Someone, originally near the top of the organization chart, may now be located further down the chart, though holding the same title, thereby revealing a decline in that person's influence or power.

Looking at the distribution of resources can tell you where the power rests within your environment. The projects with the best equipment and most supplies indicate favourites with management. These are management's pet projects and are allocated the most resources of the highest quality.

A tendency exists on projects to dedicate resources to coding while shortchanging other activities. For example, programmers receive the best equipment and better supplies while other team members receive equipment and supplies of lesser quality. This often results when the project manager has knowledge or expertise in one area but holds little appreciation of other activities. The project manager reveals his 'favourites', in this case the programmers.

Keeping alert to non-verbal clues can reveal much about the political environment. These clues cover a wide spectrum. Reading newsletters will tell you the 'favourite' people within the organization, especially if these people are constantly quoted. Continually receiving the best assignments indicates elevated status. The people who frequently participate in special, high visibility projects are approved by management.

Why do project managers have to concern themselves with what some people refer to as 'trivia'? As a project manager, you must do whatever is necessary to meet the goals and objectives of your project. Like other project managers, you must compete. These intangible clues reveal information concerning your political position relative to the others. Accurately assessing this helps your survival politically and your success as a project manager.

Political guidelines to follow

To survive politically, you need to remember these general guidelines. Keep the initiative at all times, that is, maintain momentum. Keep the project moving forward until it reaches its final goals and objectives. Slowing down the project may mean losing funds, equipment, or resources to other projects. It communicates to those in power that maybe your project lacks significance. It also gives your enemies the opportunity to gain on you.

Projects are replete with opportunities for losing momentum. Here are just a few examples: failure to gain consensus on requirements and functional specifications; inability of the team to agree on preliminary and detail design; difficulty in overlooking problems with program logic; and inability of software to satisfy requirements during testing.

Maintaining visibility is important. You must keep your project in the forefront, forever on the minds of senior management. If they forget about you and your project, management may reconsider its support for your project, with obvious consequences. You lose money, people, and equipment to other projects.

Seek a sponsor from senior management. Find someone in senior management who will provide the political muscle to turn your project into a sustaining one. Having such an important ally gives you the ability to compete effectively for resource support. You can also repel any efforts by other project managers to lower the status of your project relative to their own.

Never underestimate the power of role-playing. That means 'playing up' to the perceptions of various parties. Senior management will expect you to play a certain role and you must meet that expectation. Furthermore, the customer will expect you to perform in a certain manner, as will the team members. Any role conflict will result in some hostility towards you; after all, you breached their expectations.

Always portray the image of success, even if the project is

close to failure. Avoid revealing any panicky feelings, for instance, by constantly running to management for help or seeking the assistance of other project managers. Such behaviour only shows that you are not in control, whether over the project or yourself. The old adage 'never let them see you sweat' is as true as ever in project management. The minute your enemies – whether someone in senior management or the client or on the project team – see you displaying weakness, you will be under attack.

And finally never, repeat never, sacrifice your credibility. That does not mean telling everybody everything about your project. It does mean that you never lie. The minute you are perceived by the client, your team, or management as less than truthful, you will lose the cooperation and support needed to manage your project successfully.

Strategies for survival

In a highly political environment, there are opportunities for success or failure. Your successes depend on your abilities to exploit opportunities. As a project manager, you have several strategies that you can use to exploit circumstances. These are:

- Divide and conquer
- Cooption
- Alliance building
- Powerbrokering
- Spread responsibility
- Scapegoating
- Cooperation
- Filibustering
- Sacrifice the future for the present

Divide and conquer

This strategy is effective for dealing with the project team. Occasionally, a team member, especially if you have no formal authority over that person, will challenge your position. Using the divide and conquer strategy, you can assign tasks that have team members depending on one another to complete. Throughout the project, team members will be too busy resolving issues between themselves rather than trying to challenge or usurp your position.

For example, you may have a team member with a strong personality, someone who argues and refuses to deliver according to schedule. You can assign that person jointly with one or two other people to complete tasks, or you can assign that person to tasks where others depend on the output. Peer pressure should entice that person to complete tasks. If not, you can then use that person's behaviour as the reason for removal from the project. The danger of this strategy is that you could destroy team unity if taken to the extreme.

It is also an effective strategy for dealing with the client. If, for some reason, an important member of the client's camp is hostile towards you or the project, you should make friends with another significant party in their community. You then use that association to challenge the opposition. If the original opponent complains, you can recognize their concerns but politely mention that they do not speak for the entire organization. You want to keep them fighting among themselves rather than with you. Naturally, you must avoid being caught in the crossfire of having both sides turn on you.

You may elect to try this strategy with your own management, but do so carefully. You could play one manager against another. However, you might also find yourself on the losing side and 'out the front door' or cause indecisiveness resulting in severe delays in the project.

Cooption

With this strategy, you simply make friends with your opposition via common goals. You do that by fulfilling mutual short-term interests, thereby lessening potential damage from the opposition.

Perhaps a team member absolutely loathes working for you. To resolve that problem, you can strike a 'deal' with the employee. Tell that person, for instance, that in exchange for cooperation, you will help to enhance his or her career. Just do not promise too much, especially if you cannot be sure to deliver.

When dealing with the client, you might also find cooption useful. Perhaps the opposition in the client's side to your project has ideas for a more ambitious project. You might agree to help by slowing down the success of your project in the hope that you and your team will receive a more ambitious project. While nefarious, this tactic can lead to more lucrative work. If handled poorly, you could be without a project.

If you are having problems with a senior manager, you can try to persuade that person to think differently. Explain how the project may help solve that person's immediate pressing problems, then, the manager at least may find your project beneficial.

Alliance building

This strategy is similar to cooption but with one difference. You build a strong relationship with friends.

This strategy works well regardless of whether you make your alliance with someone on the client's side, your management's, or your project team's.

Few project managers realize the importance of making allies of other project managers. Under certain circumstances, you might make an ally of another project manager by identifying your project closely with another one.

You might do that for several reasons. You might want to associate your project with a more powerful one, hoping that you will share in its visibility. Your association with that project might also lead to greater resource allocation or at least shared resources with a favoured project.

A project might have a smaller budget and, consequently, less people and supplies than other projects. However, the project manager can tie in his project with one of the bigger ones. Some ways to achieve that is by sharing resources or providing the output of his project as the input to the bigger project.

Alliance building can prove hazardous. Being allied too closely with another project may prove detrimental especially if your ally falls into disrepute. Then you will have to disassociate your connection with that ally to protect your own project!

Powerbrokering

Here, you are taking advantage of the circumstance where two or more parties are fighting with one another. As a project manager, you can exploit this in several ways.

You can play the peacemaker. For example, two or more project managers are fighting for management's attention. You then create the image that your project is in the interests of the company while the other projects are seeking their own interests. Then you appeal to the other project managers to set aside their self-interests for the good of the company, making sure that management hears you. Management may later reward you and your project with greater visibility and more resources, even at the expense of the other projects.

Sometimes, you might avoid the role of powerbroker, especially if the odds of withstanding an onslaught from the fighting parties are minimal. You could easily find yourself in a 'Beirut' environment, where you are attacked from all sides. The key is to know when the time is right to relinquish the role of peacemaker or avoid it completely.

Spread responsibility

Periodically, you may elect to share responsibility for your project, especially if the outcome is precarious.

A common way to spread responsibility is by sharing resources with another project. Such resources might be people, equipment, and data. If something goes awry, such as a schedule slide or a decline in quality, you can attribute part of the problem to the other project using your resources.

Still another way to spread responsibility is to encourage more participation in the decision-making process. For instance, you may entice members of higher management to make critical decisions for you. Then, if the project faces problems, management will be less likely to chastise or admonish you for the results. After all their decisions contributed to the negative outcome, and they are unlikely to admonish themselves.

A common approach on projects to this is having someone assume responsibility for waiving a requirement or specification. Making a unilateral decision could prove fatal to your career. If the client refuses to yield on an impossible requirement then you can go to senior management to make the decision. That way, you keep a low profile in the entire circumstance and senior management will receive the negative pressure.

In addition, you may involve the client or your project team. Receiving their participation effectively spreads responsibility, thereby lowering the chance for complaints from either party over a particular decision.

Spreading responsibility does not absolve you from the ultimate responsibility for the outcome of the project. You alone carry that burden. But spreading responsibility can make managing your project easier. That will happen only if you spread responsibility without losing control of the project.

Scapegoating

Somewhat akin to spreading responsibility is scapegoating. It means blaming the other person for your problems, thereby absolving yourself from any responsibility. In the context of managing a project, this strategy can work very well. You simply blame someone or some organization for your project's problems.

For instance, you can blame the client for not cooperating with you. Perhaps they did not provide enough support for the project to proceed according to plan. Or you can blame senior management for not providing adequate support to complete the project successfully. This technique can prove especially useful if you had earlier identified shortcomings, and you can now point the finger at someone else rather than at yourself. You can blame poor project performance on your team or on certain members of the team.

Perhaps you were assigned people whom you did not want

in the first place but senior management forced you to accept them. You can also blame poor performance on some remote but understandable factor such as a downturn in the economy or the poor quality of employees hired into the organization. Although often quite effective, scapegoating is the tool of a weak project manager. Blaming others for your problems can easily be detected as a smokescreen for your own inadequacies as a project manager. Also, it can create enemies which is something you should try to avoid at all costs.

Cooperation

This strategy, unlike the previous one, involves making friends. Here, you help other project managers to succeed if they do the same for you. That may entail sharing scarce resources or covering for the other project manager's mistakes. It may even mean slowing the progress of your project to avoid embarrassing other project managers.

A project manager might consider lending a team member to a project that requires a certain skill. Or he might give the other project manager's team access to data, machines, facilities, etc. for a short period.

Sharing of such resources not only contributes to eliminating redundancies but also strengthens the project manager's hand. People become indebted to him.

Cooperation with the client, your management, and the project team has tremendous benefits. Each party works for the support of the other. The danger of failure, or its consequences, lessens. Mutual support rather than negative competition becomes the norm.

Yet too much cooperation can lead to mediocrity. All parties start covering for the other and negative political approaches, such as 'you scratch my back and I'll scratch yours', become more important than the projects. The consequence is extreme conformity and marginal performance. Such a collegial atmosphere will invariably frustrate the most competent and talented individuals and encourage growth of the political project manager (who may not be the most competent and talented person).

Filibustering

With this strategy, you delay progress of your project as much as possible until the delay itself becomes to your advantage or no longer becomes advantageous. For instance, you may delay your project to secure greater funding for the next fiscal year. Or you may delay your project to hurt or embarrass another project manager needing your project's output. Another reason is to avoid prematurely terminating your project, such as appearing to finish the project earlier than expected and, consequently, finding yourself seeking another project.

Filibustering works only to a point and can cause you real trouble. Unless you can attribute the delay to something everyone can relate to and they believe you, you may receive blame for the unsatisfactory performance of your project.

Sacrifice the future for the present

This strategy is employed just about everywhere, including the corporate boardroom. In the world of project management, it is also a prevalent strategy. Indeed, sacrificing the future for the present is a way of life in project management.

You may elect to reduce your resources to adjust to budget constraints and simply disregard the long range impact of your decisions. In other words, you fix the current problem and deal with the consequences later (or better yet, let your successor deal with them). Or you may make everyone work extensive overtime to meet a schedule date, knowing that later on the budget will overrun and employee turnover will rise. Thus, sacrificing the future for the present will work – for a while.

'Quick fixes' are common on projects. Due to the presence of deadlines, budget constraints, and other factors, project managers will do what they must to deliver the product to the client – hence, the deplorable quality of some products, like software. In the short run, the client gets the product within budget and on schedule. In the long run, the client has a product that only a rocket scientist could understand and a chess grandmaster could maintain.

You can face serious consequences by pursuing this strategy. Not only do you endanger the potential for a successful project but you narrow your own chances for success, too. All you are doing is placing a Bandaid on a wound when a tourniquet would be more appropriate. Usually short-term solutions lead to long-term problems on projects.

Politics is a reality

Project managers do not operate in a vacuum, void of politics. The presence of politics is inescapable in any business. The project managers who succeed are not always the best and the brightest but the ones who work smarter and not necessarily the hardest.

Admittedly, some of the strategies listed above appear sinister, even unprofessional, and they are. Yet, project managers (capable as well as inept ones) employ them every day. That does not mean you must use them. Nothing can replace project managers who are honest and direct in their dealings with their customer, their management, and their team. Nonetheless, even these project managers have to survive and, unfortunately, may have to 'use the tools of the devil to defeat him'.

Chapter 9

The people side of quality assurance

In today's project management world, the quality of workmanship, from the feasibility phase through to implementation, has become a great concern. The reasons are that poor workmanship can have dire economic, public relations, and legal implications for a company and other institutions. As a result, the importance of another function on projects – quality assurance (QA) – has increased.

Even though quality assurance makes rational sense, instituting the discipline often makes the people side of project management tense and difficult for the project manager and the quality assurance expert. Before discussing these issues, however, it is important to see how the hardside of QA works (see Figure 9.1 for tasks/responsibilites of QA).

Understanding the QA process

QA involves establishing policies, procedures, methods, and activities that ensure a product and the process of building it conforms to standards endorsed by the company and/or the industry.

But it also involves much more. It addresses meeting and exceeding customer requirements and expectations while simultaneously improving existing products, processes, and services. In addition, it entails establishing goals which are measurable and holding someone accountable for their achievement.

In some firms, a separate QA staff exists that 'audits' the quality of output of the project team. The QA staff is separate from the team. The reason is that QA people must function independently to make objective evaluations.

In other firms, a separate QA staff may not exist. Instead, one or more QA people are part of the project team. The advantage of this is that the QA people obtain an intimate understanding of the project and product. The disadvantage is that the QA people feel the pressures that everyone else on the team feels and, consequently, tend to lose their objectivity.

Regardless of whether QA personnel are part of the team or separate, the QA functions they perform remain essentially the same. They must audit the effort from start to finish by reviewing project management practices, technical workmanship, and administrative activities. For instance, they must evaluate schedule performance, look at design and construction, and review documentation such as procedures and records. To do that, however, they must develop a workable definition of quality and the objectives regarding it. They must develop measures to determine if those objectives have been met, and make objective, meaningful evaluations and recommendations for improvement.

- Establish policies, procedures, and methods
- Ensure that process(es) conforms to company standards
- Audit quality of output
- Audit project management practices
- Audit technical workmanship
- Audit administrative activities
- Provide unbiased, objective, impartial, and independent evaluations
- Develop meaningful, measurable 'quality' criteria
- Identify areas for improvement

Figure 9.1 *Tasks/responsibilities regarding the quality assurance function*

The reality of QA

That is how it is supposed to work and quite often it does. However, the experience is often so fraught with tension that managing it from a people side perspective proves difficult.

From the start, the QA function meets resistance just by virtue of its intrinsic nature. It involves reviewing another person's work. If not handled well, cooperation and communication can deteriorate.

The tension also results from pressure on the project manager to meet business conditions, such as those relating to unrealistic schedule or limited budget. When a stand-off occurs as a consequence of this situation, either the project manager or the QA staff must yield; otherwise, delays in the project occur.

Another reason tension occurs is because quality has a different meaning for each person involved – the project manager, project team, senior management, the client, and the QA experts. Unless all these people work to the same definition, tension will be the norm rather than the exception.

Perhaps the most important reason for the tension, however, is that the client, senior management, project team, and the project manager operate from different perspectives. Unless those perspectives can be harmonized, tension over QA issues will arise (see Figure 9.2).

Client perspective

The client wants everything to meet all its requirements, even those addressing quality. It also wants the product as soon as possible, especially if it hopes to improve productivity and performance. Yet it wants a top quality product. Delivering a product sooner than planned can conflict with the need to develop a high quality product. Everyone on the project will take shortcuts regarding schedule, budget, and technical criteria. That results frequently in doing rework, performing 'patchwork' on code, and overlooking technical problems. Of course, as a result, quality starts to deteriorate.

PROJECT MANAGER

- Defines quality assurance roles and responsibilities
- Eliminates waste
- Engenders an atmosphere of teamwork
- Fosters total participation among all parties
- Works with vendors
- Identifies quantitative measurable acceptable 'quality' objectives
- Demonstrates sincere attitude towards quality assurance problem identification and resolution

SENIOR MANAGEMENT

- Encourage open discussions
- Guarantee job security
- Promote policies that consistently stimulate the 'want' to improve

CLIENT

- Ensures continuity of management practices for product delivery
- Pursues improved quality and productivity
- Supports all parties through total participation

PROJECT TEAM

- Works closely with client representatives
- Strives toward continuous improvement
- Eliminates waste
- Supports goals of organization

Figure 9.2 *Tasks/responsibilities regarding quality assurance*

Senior management perspective

Senior management want to maintain the organization's reputation for delivering useful, reliable products. At the same time, they want to deliver the products on time and within budget. Essentially, they want the best of both worlds.

Yet delivering reliable, useful products within budget and on time sets the stage for conflict, especially when technical problems start to appear. When there is conflict, senior management yields to the pressure of meeting the schedule or budget. Once again, quality starts to deteriorate.

Project team perspective

Many project team members do not like to comply with standards. After all, they say, the real objective is delivering a product that works, not complying with standards. To do that, they require autonomy – independence – to develop creative solutions to problems.

In addition, many team members do not like the idea of knowing that someone is checking their work. It implies a lack of confidence in their performance and judgement. Professionals police themselves, not some regulatory body.

Such perspectives lead to all sorts of ways to circumvent QA. Team members start 'fudging' or even lying in their reports. Others avoid responsibility, and some even start pointing fingers at people for causing problems, including QA personnel. And again, quality starts to deteriorate.

QA perspective

QA people (like the project team, senior management, and the client) have their own perspectives. Basically, they want to ensure that all standards have been met. That means identifying and preventing the costs associated with poor quality, such as legal liability, lost business, and theft. QA, therefore, must look at all aspects of a project, including the management of business, behavioural, and technical processes. If at any point it detects a serious problem, QA must blow the whistle even in the face of displeasure from certain parties. Failure to do so might allow for inferior quality workmanship and could place the client and even the entire company at high risk.

Project manager perspective

As usual, the project manager is in the centre, having to wrestle with all the other perspectives while at the same time delivering a product on time and within budget. He must somehow satisfy them all but in reality must compromise. That is, he finds himself concurring with some parties rather than others. As a general rule, however, when pressure becomes intense, the project manager quite often neglects one or more activities. Given a choice, he more than likely will ignore the QA activities.

The project manager makes this decision for three reasons. He knows that the immediate impact of not delivering a product on time and within budget is much greater than not addressing the QA requirements. Also, ignoring a QA requirement may not affect his career. QA-related problems often surface in the future, and he will more than likely not be the manager responsible at that time for maintaining the product but will be managing another project. Finally, QA activities take considerable time away from the work that builds a product and quality starts to deteriorate.

Strategies for managing QA

Fortunately, you can reduce the possibility of meeting such problems in the following ways.

First, work with the QA people to obtain a mutually acceptable definition of quality before the project starts. The client and senior management should also participate in this.

Developing an acceptable definition is not however enough. You will also need to develop mutually acceptable objectives to measure how well the project is meeting quality assurance requirements.

Second, mutually define the role and involvement level of QA. Determine answers to questions like: Should QA be part of the project team or independent from it? Should QA personnel attend meetings? If so, which ones and what should be their participation level? When should QA become involved in a project?

Third, plan for QA involvement. Your time and cost estimates should account for this. The flowtime, or duration, of activities should also reflect QA participation and decisions. If QA finds problems, therefore, you will not have to make a dramatic adjustment to your budget and schedule because you have already planned for that circumstance.

Fourth, treat QA staff as members of the project team even if they are not. Communicate with QA staff; put a stop to any 'games' by team members that seek to keep QA people isolated and uninformed. All that achieves is to raise suspicions on the part of the QA people and engender hostility. Then the project develops an atmosphere of 'us' against 'them'.

Fifth, become an advocate of QA by stressing its importance to the success of the project. At all meetings emphasize the need to comply with QA requirements and follow up on how well compliance has occurred. If QA discovers a problem and suggests immediate correction, give it your sincere attention.

Teamwork

QA must play an instrumental role in projects. If QA does not fulfill that role then the likelihood of the product exposing the company to risk increases.

As a project manager, therefore, you want the QA function to contribute positively to your project. For that to happen, you must take the necessary steps to ensure that the people side of project management proceeds as smoothly as possible. The answer is teamwork.

PART III

Working with the players

Chapter 10

The foundation of
teamwork

As a project manager an important responsibility is to manage your project team. Your team comprises people with varying backgrounds. Some may be university graduates while others may have school education. Some may have fifteen years of experience while others may have less than six months. Some members may be specialists while others are generalists. You must ensure that all these people perform up to and beyond minimum requirements.

To make that happen, you should provide an environment that encourages people to perform well. That means removing the obstacles that frustrate and disenchant team members. These obstacles can be divided into two categories: physical and non-physical. Dealing with the first category involves eliminating the tangible factors that impede productivity. These may include crowded office space, antiquated computing equipment, and dimly lit offices. These and other physical obstacles can hinder performance, and you must do everything in your power to remove such obstacles.

The second category of obstacles is more difficult to handle. They are hard to identify and resolve, yet these factors can damage productivity greatly. They come in many forms: people with inadequate skills and training, interference in the project by different levels of management, and low morale are a few of the non-physical factors that can negatively affect productivity.

The ideal is to create an environment that encourages people to perform. That may sound easy, but it is hard to do in reality. Obstacles will always confront the project team and much depends on how well you handle them. The best way is to eliminate as many as possible.

To remove both physical and non-physical barriers, you must accomplish several tasks:

- building a solid organizational structure
- selecting the right people for project leaders
- eliminating barriers to communication
- improving the physical work environment
- managing and leading team members

Building an organizational structure

Today, the matrix organizational structure is commonplace. Using a matrix, as shown in Figure 10.1, an organization can have people from different functional groups, such as accounting or data processing, support the project manager. These people may also support another project. Consequently, they work on more than one project and usually for more than one project manager. This clearly violates the unity of command principle.

The consequences of using a matrix structure can be serious. People become confused over which project manager to support and whether they should obey their functional boss or the project manager. The likelihood of placing a team member in such conflict increases and the opportunity for team unity can rapidly crumble.

The matrix structure offers, nonetheless, several advantages, otherwise, many Fortune 500 firms would not adopt it. It provides a company with adaptability to changing market conditions without having to lay off people. It also allows sharing of people with rare, highly specialized skills among different projects.

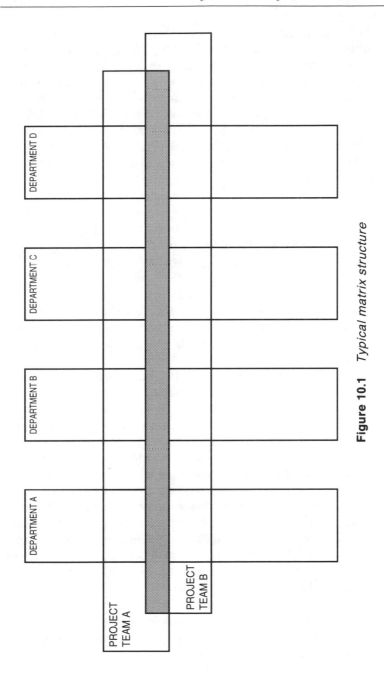

Figure 10.1 *Typical matrix structure*

Software development projects, for example, face these two problems all the time. Firms offering computing products to the public must adapt to changing market conditions. Developing a stand-alone word processing or database application package for the mainframe environment, for example, may no longer prove competitive and the company must develop another type of integrated package to remain competitive.

Computing projects often require people with highly specialized skills. They need people that can program using from first to fifth generation languages, or can use certain computer aided software engineering (CASE) tools.

To offset some of the negative effects of the matrix structure, some firms have employed task forces. These are teams devoted entirely to one project until complete. Figure 10.2 illustrates a typical task force structure within an organization.

The task force offers several advantages. It maintains unity of command because everyone involved reports to the task force coordinator, or project manager, for the entire length of the project. People can also concentrate on one project rather than supporting several simultaneously.

After completing the project, the task force dissolves and members report to their functional managers, support other projects, or move to another task force. Once the project is over, team members are on their own once again. These people, or their functional managers, must find work for them since the original task force exists no more.

Whether your project exists in an environment which uses matrix or task force structures, you must establish the right organizational structure within your project. Before building the organizational structure, keep two concepts in mind.

As a project manager you can only control so many people. The number of people directly supporting you should not exceed ten. Beyond that number, controlling the project becomes difficult. Your only options are to scale down the number of people supporting you, or to add project leaders. If you have less than seven people, a leader is not required. The concept of determining how many people you can effectively control is called span of control. Trying to handle too many

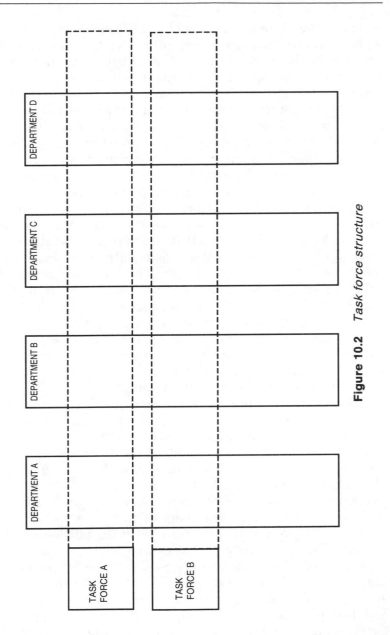

Figure 10.2 *Task force structure*

people can result in management by reaction; having a leader with a team of fewer than seven people leads to overcontrol and a needless layer of management. Figure 10.3 illustrates using span of control to improve the structure of your organization.

Unity of command is another important managerial principle to know. Theoretically, a person should have only one boss. That is, the people who work for you during the project work for no one else. The idea is that no person can serve two masters. For the most part that is true in functional organizations and where people work on one major project.

Figure 10.4 displays a typical organizational chart for a project. At the top is the project manager responsible for the project. You will also notice that the chart shows two team leaders, primarily because the number of people other than the project manager is 10 so this division is required. In addition, you can see beneath the project manager box a dashed line indicating external support to the project. This external support box can be positioned just about anywhere on the chart, reflecting its level of importance to the project. Figures 10.5 and 10.6 reflect alternatives to show the reporting relationship between external support and the project.

The organizational chart is an important tool. You should prepare one before project activities begin. Publishing the organizational chart communicates responsibilities and clarifies reporting relationships. If you want a useful organizational chart, you should draft it to address the functional needs of the project, not the politics. Organizational charts often reflect the political composition of large projects with a different version published just about every month. More than the names in the boxes have been changed; the entire structure has been rearranged and has no relevance to the mission of the project. Constantly revising the organizational chart to reflect political considerations only breeds bad feelings among employees and shows a poor sense of direction by the project manager. So, revise your organizational chart sparingly.

When publishing the organizational chart, ensure that everyone receives a copy. That way everyone knows their responsibilities and reporting relationships.

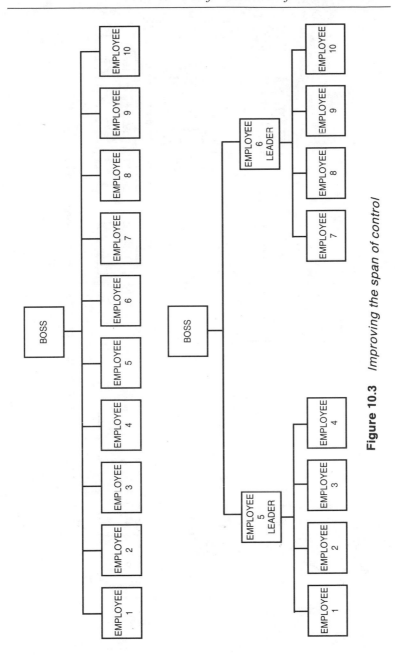

Figure 10.3 *Improving the span of control*

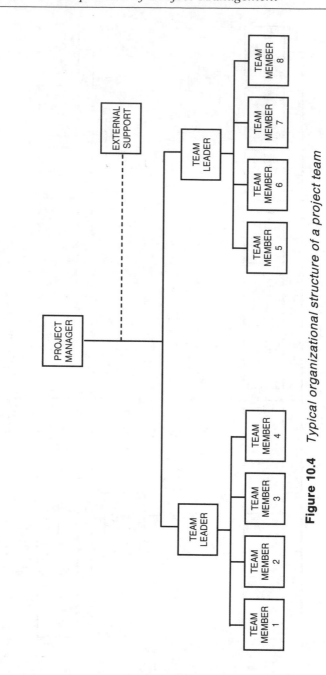

Figure 10.4 *Typical organizational structure of a project team*

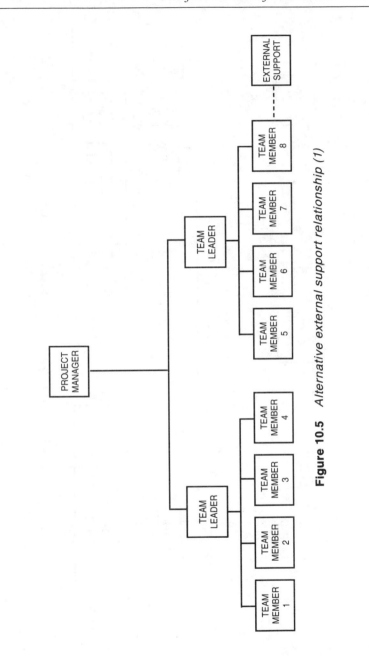

Figure 10.5 *Alternative external support relationship (1)*

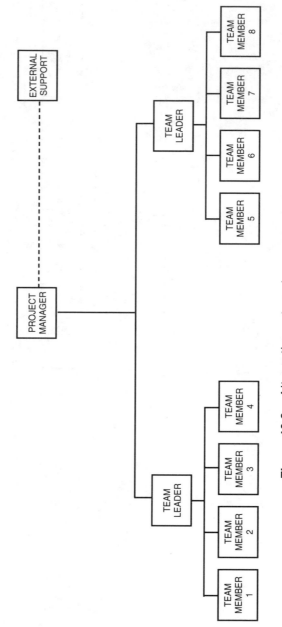

Figure 10.6   *Alternative external support relationship (2)*

Selecting the leader

As mentioned earlier, if your project has more than ten people you should incorporate leaders to maintain effective span of control. A leader is a person you designate to assist you in managing the project. This does not absolve you from responsibility nor does the leader make all the decisions; rather, the leader is the person you rely upon to execute your decisions.

What qualities should you look for in a leader? A good candidate for the position is someone who is enthusiastic, a person who goes that extra mile. Enthusiasm infects other people. Coupled with enthusiasm is having a positive attitude, a feeling of 'can do'.

But enthusiasm is not enough. The candidate must have good communication skills. Although speaking and writing are important, an effective leader should also be a good listener to assess objectively the progress of the project. Closely allied to this characteristic is good interpersonal relationship skills. Leaders lacking these skills, such as the ability to empathize and see things from different perspectives, will face continual problems with the other team members.

Your leader should have the respect of peers, yourself, your management, and your client. This respect is vitally important because the leader has less authority, specified or implied, than you. Without that respect, the leader will be merely a symbol and your chain of command will deteriorate.

The candidate should also be able to function autonomously while simultaneously following instructions. The leader should function, therefore, with minimal direction so you can concentrate on other matters.

Finally, your candidate should have good technical knowledge and skills but does not have to be the best on the team. The candidate must have the requisite knowledge and skills to keep abreast of activities. Without that knowledge, despite being a human relations genius, the leader will function with great difficulty. The more technical the project, the more knowledgeable and skilful your leader should be in the subject area.

In summary, you want someone who can function in your place if you are absent. This important consideration allows you to manage the project rather than letting the project manage you.

Eliminating barriers to communication

Poor communications is a leading cause of unsatisfactory project performance. Numerous barriers exist to good communications and effective project managers know how to overcome them.

One common communication barrier is having unclearly defined lines of authority. For instance, people do not know who reports to whom and under what circumstances. Everyone may know who the project manager is but no one may know who is the leader or which leader to follow. An excellent way to overcome this problem is by developing and publishing an organizational chart.

Another common barrier is poor role definition. People do not know who is responsible for performing which tasks. They either duplicate the effort of others or stand around in a quandary wondering what to do next. An organizational chart is an effective way to overcome this barrier, but not the only way.

How often do different team members interview the same person when collecting information regarding requirements? How often do team members develop similar output to go into the final product? These and other circumstances occur quite frequently on projects. And they increase as the project develops in scope and effort.

The Employee Assignment form, shown in Figure 10.7, is an excellent way to communicate people's responsibilities and tasks on a project. You simply list each team member's tasks and provide them with a copy of the listing. You can use the form in Figure 10.7 by matching the applicable number below with the corresponding one located in the form:

1. The last name, first name, and middle initial of the person to work on the activity
2. The clock number or social security number of the employee, if necessary
3. The numeric designation uniquely identifying the activity

EMPLOYEE NAME	EMPLOYEE NUMBER	ACTIVITY NUMBER	ACTIVITY DESCRIPTION	TOTAL HOURS TO COMPLETE	EARLY START DATE	EARLY FINISH DATE	CO-WORKERS
(1)	(2)	(3)	(4)	(5)	(6)	(7)	(8)

Figure 10.7   *Employee Assignment form*

TASKS / NAMES	CLEAR SITE	CONDUCT SURVEY	ROUGH GRADE	PREPARE CONCRETE MIXING AREA	TRANSPORT CRANE TO SITE	ASSEMBLE CRANE
SMITH	X			X	X	X
JONES						X
WEBSTER			X		X	X
COCHRAN				X		X
GEBHARDT		X				X
WILLIAMS					X	X

Figure 10.8　*Responsibility matrix*

4. A short narrative description of the activity
5. The total hours estimated to perform the task
6. The earliest time that the activity can begin
7. The earliest time that the activity can finish
8. The last names of the other employees to work on the activity.

A reason exists for giving the employees the earliest dates. It forces them not to procrastinate. If they know the float or the late dates, they may elect not to complete tasks in the earliest possible time. This technique reflects Parkinson's Law, that a task will consume the time available for its completion. If you say a task will take 100 hours to complete, for example, then that is the time people on the project will likely take. If you say 1000 hours, then that is the time they will take.

If you do not like using the form, you can develop a responsibility matrix. You can also use the matrix as a supplement to the form. The matrix lists all the tasks and people involved in the project. Where the two axes intersect indicates the responsibilities for performing the tasks. Figures 10.8 and 10.9 are two examples of how to design a responsibility matrix.

The form or the matrix offers two effective ways to over-

NAMES / TASKS	SMITH	JONES	WEBSTER	COCHRAN	GEBHARDT	WILLIAMS
CLEAR SITE	X					
CONDUCT SURVEY					X	
ROUGH GRADE			X			
PREPARE CONCRETE MIXING AREA	X			X		
TRANSPORT CRANE TO SITE	X		X			X
ASSEMBLE CRANE	X	X	X	X	X	X

Figure 10.9 *Responsibility matrix (alternative format)*

come obstacles to communication, but to realize the benefit that everyone must receive an updated copy.

Another common obstacle to good communications is unclear goals and objectives. Frequently, project managers fail to inform everyone of what the project aims to achieve. By knowing the goals and objectives of their project, team members can orient their behaviour and performance accordingly. The goals and objectives also offer employees motivation for doing their part if they can see the meaning of their work. In other words, it offers a vision. People can then use the goals and objectives to build a communications bridge between them and all the other team members.

One way to have people focus on the goals and objectives of your project is to distribute a copy of the Statement of Work. Or you can print in large type on a piece of paper the overall mission and objectives of the project. Team members can place this on their desk to remind them of the mission of the project. Regardless of the method, ensure that people always focus on the overall goals and objectives of the project, otherwise, they will quickly go in separate directions.

Jargon, especially on technical projects, is a leading obstacle to effective communications. Acronyms and abbreviations, for example, are commonplace. Many data processing professionals, for example, use jargon in their work. Systems analysts, programmers, database administrators, and the like have their own set of terms, acronyms, and abbreviations. Such language can prove difficult to understand, even incomprehensible. In fact, even team members may find difficulty in understanding each other. Unless everyone, including new members of the project team, knows what the jargon means, communication will be difficult.

The temptation to use jargon is an interesting phenomenon. Some people use it to impress other people with their level of knowledge while others use it as a smoke-screen to conceal their ignorance of a subject. Whatever the reason, jargon should be avoided.

If you have a project which requires considerable jargon, consider developing a glossary. It will lessen the opportunities for misunderstanding. The project handbook is a good place for the glossary.

Lack of, or inadequate, documentation is another barrier to good communications. This documentation can range from forms to procedures. To many people, documentation smacks of red tape and administrative burdens. Sometimes that may be true. More often, however, some team members simply avoid preparing documentation or even referring to it, which allows the opportunity for poor communications to occur. ·

To resolve this problem, ensure that people have access to, or copies of, all project documentation. However, that is not enough. You need to encourage people to use the documentation – which means instilling discipline. For example whenever a question arises, you should say something like, 'Well, what does it say in the project procedures?' or 'Did you complete the necessary form?' By instilling this discipline, the documentation will serve as an effective communications medium.

Lack of meetings or poorly run ones are common barriers to effective communication. People often attend meetings without having any idea of the results, or the meetings become argumentative sessions.

Meetings themselves do not improve communication. Having the right meetings and running them correctly does improve communications. To ensure effective use of meetings, make it standard operating procedure to have meetings only when necessary, such as after completing a major phase or sub-product, and prepare an agenda for each meeting to enforce self-discipline.

Lack of adequate tools and facilities also impedes effective communication. In data processing shops, for example, people often use incompatible equipment. The burdensome task of translating information from one computer to another is required to enable two or more people to communicate, and this increases the chance of miscommunication. Another example is offices with too few telephones. Occasionally, five or more people must share a phone that is constantly in use. People become frustrated and angry with each other. They may avoid using the phone, becoming reluctant to communicate with people outside the office.

People need the tools and facilities to do their job. Without that support, barriers to effective communication are inevitable. You may not be able to remove all the barriers, but you can facilitate better communications.

Unresolved negative conflict is the final major barrier to effective communications. People build walls between themselves and others, resulting in poor or no communications with each other. Allowing this to continue or leaving it to gradually fade away will decimate productivity. Despite the adverse effects of the situation continuing, many project managers avoid conflict resolution due to its unpleasantness. But they will also find the consequences of the continuing conflict very unpleasant. The real issue is whether to address the problem now or face a much more severe one later.

The project manager makes the difference

Productive teams are those where people work harmoniously together. But that can only happen if you, the project manager, engender such an environment; no one else can do that and no one else has the responsibility to make that happen.

Chapter 11

Leading individual team members

The way you lead people can have tremendous impact on the amount and quality of your team's productivity. Your management style can dramatically affect your people's attitude towards you and your project.

Effectively leading your team requires two interrelated styles. On the one hand, you must deal with individual team members; on the other, you must handle the team as a single entity. In the end, you must find a way to harmonize these, otherwise, you will face problems both with individuals and the team as a whole. In this chapter, you will learn how to handle individual team members.

When leading individuals, successful project managers will consider the following areas:

1. Getting the right people
2. Knowing which incentives to use
3. Dealing with 'difficult' people
4. Encouraging creativity from individuals
5. Delegating effectively
6. Taking advantage of training

Getting the right people

Project managers often select people (if they have that option) for only one or two reasons. Typically, they choose someone

- Inaccurate cost benefit analysis
- Poor design
- Output not corresponding to design
- Impractical product design
- Poor quality
- Inappropriate product testing criteria
- Incorrect alternative chosen
- Unrealistic specifications
- Communication breakdown
- Product delivered does not match expectations
- Technology unavailable (poor timing)
- Incomplete models or prototypes
- Configuration management not available

Figure 11.1 *Possible adverse results of choosing people lacking in the three factors: education, personality, or experience*

who they feel is technically proficient. That is they can do the tasks required by the position.

Although technical proficiency is important, it is not the only consideration. The most technically proficient person may be lacking in other areas that could result in lower productivity. For instance, they may lack a complete understanding of the project life cycle, the importance of documentation and training or of maintaining cooperative relations with the client.

As a project manager, you must consider three other factors: education, experience, and personality. Figure 11.1 lists some of the adverse results of choosing someone lacking in these areas.

Education can affect the way a person performs, regardless of technical proficiency. Someone, for example, may be proficient in a technical area but lack the education to understand how that expertise fits in to the entire project. Or they may only know how to do something really well one way, such as mechanical or electrical engineering or programming. Of course, the person should have the appropriate level of education to work on the project. Yet education alone is not enough. The educational degree may not be related to what is happening on the project.

Experience can also influence a person's performance.

Ideally, you want to hire the most experienced person. However, that criterion may prove troublesome, especially if it is the sole criterion. Experience may mean that someone has done something a particular way for many years and is not aware of, nor cares about, new approaches. Some project managers misconstrue age as evidence of proficiency. Ironically, a person may work for several years in a specialized field but never reach a high level of expertise: Someone much younger may be more proficient.

Personality is the final area to consider. How people react to their environment can profoundly influence a team's productivity. Some people have the appropriate education, technical proficiency, and experience but lack the type of personality required to perform certain tasks on a project. Placing people in a sales position who have the technical proficiency, education, and experience but not the right personality may cause problems for them and the project, and they may be unable to cope with the requirements of the job.

Take the common example of someone who is a top-notch programmer in COBOL, worked for a Fortune 500 firm in this capacity, and received a degree in computer science from a leading university. Yet he never worked directly for a client. Now he has been promoted to lead programmer-analyst because of his technical background, overlooking his lack of listening and interpersonal relations skills. Six months later, the morale and performance of the team has declined and the relationship with the client has deteriorated.

When considering the personality of the individual, you should ask yourself not only will that person's personality match the job but will it mesh with your project team's and with your own? Ideally, you want someone whose personality will fit with your own, the team's, and the requirements of the job – and not necessarily in that order.

In summary, always consider technical proficiency, experience, personality, and education. Relying on just one variable can lead to a mismatch between the person and the job, resulting in a decline in productivity.

Knowing which incentives to use

Some project managers feel that they have little power to influence team members. More often than not, they hope people will feel rewarded by the job itself. Project managers often feel this way, especially if they work in a matrix environment where they lack command and control over the people. They cannot grant pay rises or punish people, at least directly.

Yet project managers, regardless of the environment, are not helpless. They can use both positive and negative incentives.

Positive incentives are often called 'the carrot'. You use these incentives to stimulate people to improve their productivity or to reward them for outstanding performance. For example, you can send people on training courses to improve their level of expertise, thereby increasing their contribution to the project. Indeed, some team members see training as a 'perk' for doing a good job.

You can send team members, depending on their field of expertise, to annual conventions, in-house courses, seminars, and workshops. The best approach, of course, is to blend the team member's needs with the project's.

Providing more challenging work assignments is another positive incentive. You can switch people to more challenging tasks after they master easier ones. This is known as job enrichment.

Junior team members can progress to more difficult assignments, perhaps working on a component of the product. Technical specialists can handle leadership responsibilities or more challenging assignments that force them to 'stretch'. Stretching means that the person handles a task or tackles a goal requiring a little more effort than usual.

Another effective incentive is allowing an individual to participate in the decision-making process. When making an important decision that affects a particular individual, you can ask that person for ideas and suggestions. Even though you may not agree with all the ideas and suggestions, you will communicate that you value that person's opinion.

Technical professionals, on average, are well educated.

Many are university graduates. They can think logically as well as analyse and solve problems. That leads to a desire to participate in the decision-making process. If they feel like mere instruments of production rather than valuable contributors, their performance will decline or they may depart or both. By having them participate in the decision-making process, they will feel part of a team.

Giving compensatory time off can spur an improvement in performance. This often serves as a reward for working long hours under abnormal circumstances. People can then use this time as desired.

It is an excellent motivator for programmers and other team members who work long hours over a short period of time to complete a sub-product or product. For example, they may work to build components of a product for delivery the next day. Upon making that delivery, they can relax when the workload lessens.

Recognition provides another powerful incentive. Many individuals will do almost anything to receive approval from people in important positions; as a result, they will go that extra mile. As a project manager, you will want to recognize those who have provided outstanding performance. An effective way to do that is to write letters of appreciation and commendation for placement in the individual's personnel file. Even a simple comment to the person's boss can have a powerful impact.

You might consider, recognizing engineers for technical excellence for designing and building a component of an automobile or aircraft, or programmers on a data processing project for building a well-structured program.

Not all incentives are positive; some are negative. Even if you lack direct control over someone, you can still use the 'stick'. You can talk to the employee's functional boss about their poor performance and even recommend drastic action. You can terminate the employee's participation on the project. You can assign the employee to less challenging tasks. Finally, you can deny the employee certain privileges, such as reducing or disallowing attendance at seminars and workshops.

You should place your emphasis on positive rather than

negative incentives. The former tends to have a more lasting effect than the latter. However, you should employ positive incentives only when necessary. Some project managers use positive incentives too frequently, thereby diluting their impact. In addition, you want to use negative incentives sparingly; otherwise, you will find people resentful and only performing minimally.

Dealing with difficult people

Not everyone on your team will function as the perfect employee. You cannot satisfy everyone and some employees are just never happy. Difficult people can make your job as a project manager very tough.

Difficult people come in a number of forms. There is the rebellious type who refuses to cooperate under any circumstances. Akin to this type is the argumentative person. These people constantly disagree with you and everybody else just for the sake of disagreeing. The only difference between them and the rebellious type is that the former usually cooperates with you in the end. There is also the employee with the negative attitude. This person never has a kind word about you or your project; his or her negative attitude eventually becomes infectious.

At the other end of the spectrum are two other difficult types of employees. These are the quiet, non-assertive team members and those who have resigned from the project even though still physically present. The quiet, non-assertive ones are difficult because you must continually goad or prod them into action. The resigned ones are even more difficult because their responses for not doing anything are usually unrelated to you. For example they may not have wanted to work on your project but were assigned anyway.

Handling people at both ends of the spectrum is extremely difficult. It is possible, however, to alleviate or rectify your relationship with these employees.

First, identify the source of the problem. Try to ascertain why they behave the way they do. That does not mean being a psychiatrist but it does mean trying to discover whether you are the cause of the problem. If you are not the cause, then you cannot totally change the person's attitude.

Next, meet in private with the person and use effective listening skills. A private conversation with the individual often reveals the source of the problem. You have the opportunity to break down the barriers between yourself and that person by listening rather than doing all the talking.

Third, be honest and straightforward. Let the person know your feelings about his or her behaviour. Inform that person about the impact his or her behaviour has on the project. Cite specifics, not generalities, and let the individual know that such behaviour is not acceptable.

Fourth, do not hesitate to employ positive or negative incentives. Learn, however, to use them sparingly; otherwise they will later become ineffectual. Above all, if you promise something then follow through. Do not mislead or you will have a serious morale problem that could spread to other members of the project team.

Fifth, rather than using negative incentives, try to direct difficult people's energies into tasks appropriate to their personality. Use these tasks to harness their energy. You will find that changing their behaviour is very difficult and no project manager (even a psychiatrist) can do it overnight. The best that you can do is work with them by giving them work suitable to their personality. You do not want to assign rebellious people, for example, to tasks requiring cooperation with other people. Nor do you want to assign taciturn employees to tasks requiring considerable social interaction and public speaking.

Sixth, apply peer pressure. If someone behaves inappropriately, let their peers handle the situation. Peers can effectively send subtle messages to colleagues without the supervisor ever intervening. Temporary ostracism and accusations are two effective ways in which groups discipline members. Quite often, difficult people will alter their behaviour when they feel pressure from you and the group. That is because people have a need for social acceptance.

Dealing with difficult people is not easy. Just about every project manager finds it an unpleasant, agonizing experience.

- Intelligent
- Experimenting
- Visionary
- Un-prejudiced
- Open-minded
- Determined
- Imaginative
- Intuitive
- Energetic
- Independent
- Risk-taker
- Curious
- Simplifier
- Flexible
- Achiever

Figure 11.2   *Characteristics of a creative person*

Yet you must deal with it or your project will face great difficulties.

Encouraging creativity from individual team members

Most people do not enjoy performing the same task repeatedly. They want variety, and they want to be creative. The idea that only certain people are creative is a myth. Most psychologists and psychiatrists agree that everyone can be creative (see Figure 11.2 for the characteristics of creative people). What hinders creativity is the social environment, which inhibits any sense of creativity through the pressure to conform. As a project manager, however, you want people to be creative so you can concentrate on managing the project. There are several measures you can take to encourage creativity in employees.

Giving an individual sufficient job autonomy is one effective way. Do not dictate step-by-step how a person should perform a job – you might just as well do the job yourself. You may of course have to define everything at the start for a new employee. As that person matures on the project, however, you can allow him or her to work more independently.

By the very nature of their work, technical professionals function autonomously. They must often produce alone and then possibly review it with their peers. If standards exist, they must comply with them; however, they still 'compose' autonomously. If project managers intervene on *how to* rather than *what to*, they will impede the creativity of the team members.

To be creative, people also need the right quantity and quality of equipment and supplies. Using antiquated equipment or having insufficient supplies can make it very difficult to be creative. Employees will become frustrated and will do only the minimum to complete their tasks.

Take the example of design engineers and draughtsmen drawing by hand diagrams of parts for a new commuter aircraft. Nothing is more frustrating than revising and redrawing these diagrams to ensure their accuracy. However with a CAD/CAM (computer-aided design/computer-aided manufacturing) system, the diagrams are updated automatically once the revisions have been entered.

Pressures from outside the project environment can stifle creativity so you must take measures to isolate your people from them. Naturally, you will be unable to protect them from all outside pressures, such as higher management dicta on doing business or countless administrative hassles smacking of red tape. Such outside pressure not only affects the creativity of team members but the project manager as well, but you must try to protect your team from outside pressures as much as possible to preclude stifling creativity.

You can also encourage creativity by generating an atmosphere of 'freedom to fail' rather than one of a 'freedom to succeed'. Failure to succeed should not be a crime. People need the latitude to take chances; penalizing someone for failure inhibits anyone from taking chances.

Software development projects, for example, require a freedom to fail atmosphere more than most other types of projects. That is because too many unknown variables exist, such as complexity of logic and relationship with other program modules. That requires experimentation which, in turn, necessitates taking chances.

You should encourage team members to experiment with different ways of tackling tasks. If they fail, encourage them to learn from the experience. Unfortunately, many environments have a freedom to succeed atmosphere that discourages creativity. The result is a project filled with cautious, even non-assertive, people fearful of trying something different.

Still another way to encourage creativity is by involving individuals in decision-making. People will feel they have a personal stake in the outcome and thus have a willingness to provide creative ideas on making it happen.

Asking team members, for example, how best to do something will make them feel that not only have they a say over their destiny but also over that of their project. They can not then fail to maintain an active interest in the progress of their project.

Finally, promote stretching, by giving people challenging tasks. Simply completing a task, for instance, is not enough; employees have to complete it according to a standard. You or someone else may have established the standard but it must be one that encourages them to do their best. As they strive to do their best, they cannot help but be creative.

One of the biggest threats to creativity in the project arena is the 'paint-by-numbers' approach towards building products. From a business perspective, ideas of modularized components make excellent sense. For the most part, these approaches have helped to reduce costs and speed up development. To creative people, however, the restrictions that they impose can prove bothersome and constrain the freedom necessary to develop original solutions. Project managers, therefore, must strike a balance between encouraging the creativity of team members and meeting the business needs of the project and the client.

Creativity is crucial to completing a project successfully because unpredictable circumstances always arise that will require creative solutions. Failure to appreciate the role of creativity in a project can result in delays or worse.

Delegating effectively

Project managers cannot do everything themselves; otherwise they would sit at their desk for more than eight hours each day for seven days a week.

Yet some project managers try to do everything themselves, and that includes doing the technical work. The consequence is an overworked, burnt-out project manager and employees who feel bored, insignificant, and angry.

You cannot do everything yourself unless you are working on a one-person project. You will find it, therefore, in your interest to delegate. Team members will also find it beneficial. Your delegation of duties gives them the opportunity to pursue greater responsibilities, appreciate your own tasks, and feel like active participants in the project.

When delegating, consider the personality of the person who will do the work. This person should have the appropriate personality to do the job. For instance, do not delegate customer liaison responsibilities to an employee who enjoys working alone and is an introvert. Always delegate tasks that match a person's personality.

Some people, for example, make superb engineers but fail miserably when dealing with people. They can design and build efficient and effective systems but lack patience and interpersonal skills. Likewise, former sales people who have an understanding of engineering concepts and practices may still fail as engineers because they lack the technical 'instinct' required.

Furthermore, try to delegate tasks to people who have the capability, experience, education, and ability to do them well. Avoid delegating a task to someone totally unprepared to handle it.

Remember, delegation does not absolve you of responsibility. You are designating someone to act on your behalf. You should give the person to whom you have delegated work the authority to perform on your behalf. That includes giving them the freedom and backing to make decisions in your absence. Delegating without authority is like having a managerial position without money or staff; you would find it virtually impossible to accomplish anything.

You should also follow up on what you have delegated. The best way is by talking with the employee to determine progress. But follow-up conversation communicates more than an interest in progress. It also shows that you are interested in the employee and that what you have delegated is important. In other words, you show that you care.

Finally, when you delegate ensure that you communicate

clearly your requirements, goals, objectives, and expectations about the tasks. Do not just delegate with little or no background information. That shows a lack of interest on your part and indicates your inability to handle the tasks yourself. You do not want to leave the employee with a negative impression about why you are delegating in the first place; that kills motivation.

Taking advantage of training

Although few project managers realize it, they have a powerful tool for motivating employees: training. Unfortunately, some project managers, even functional managers, view training as a vacation for the employee. That attitude is harmful both for the individual and the entire project. It shows that these project managers care little for the growth of the people supporting them.

Successful project managers have a different attitude towards training. They see it as a mechanism for increasing employee growth and productivity. They also realize that some employees abuse training. To ensure that training becomes a vital part of your project, there are a number of factors to consider.

You should send people only to relevant training, which directly relates to their work. Sending people to training remotely connected to their work is neither productive nor cost-effective. For example, sending team members to training on another subject will not prove cost-effective, especially if they will never apply that knowledge. Similarly sending team members to a course on using a specific analytical technique which is never applied is not cost-effective.

Remember that a loss of productivity occurs, at least temporarily, when a person attends a training course. Hopefully, they will become more productive as a result of having attended that training.

The best place to have training is offsite, unless it is on-the-job training (OJT). The workplace is the worse site for training because interruptions occur, thereby disrupting the learning process. Trainees returning to their workstations are easily pulled away to work on daily tasks, sometimes never to return to the training course.

But you can use training to your advantage. When slow periods occur, you can send people on training courses. While in training, people can improve themselves, whereas, if they sit idle for any time, they become mischievous and disrupt busy team members.

It is useful to send people on training courses as a reward for good, not bad, performance. Some project managers send poor performers to get them out of the way. This approach has disastrous consequences. The good employees see themselves as being taken advantage of; the bad employees see it as reinforcing bad performance. As a result the good employees become demoralized and productivity declines.

Once team members return from training, allow them time to apply their newly acquired skills and knowledge. This gives them an opportunity to reinforce their learning and discover ways to improve their productivity. As the team members apply the skills and knowledge and experience success, other employees become eager first for the training and then to apply their new expertise. In the end, everyone gains – you, the team member, and the company all become winners.

Finally, do not hesitate to explore the different ways to train people. Training courses are just one medium. Others include OJT, computer-based training (CBT), and self-development (such as books). All of these will work under the right circumstances.

Building an effective team

Your people are your most important ingredients for a successful project. How you lead them will have a powerful influence on the outcome. Remember, you manage activities but you lead people. Too often, project managers manage people like objects such as a schedule or microcomputer. That is unfortunate because it is people who make the project happen.

Chapter 12

Motivating the entire team

Not only must you lead individuals, you must also lead the entire team as a cohesive unit. Your leadership style with the group can have a positive or detrimental effect. A project manager may be skilled in handling individuals but perform ineffectively with the team as a whole. You must balance both sides with each other. Only then will you become an effective leader and manager.

When leading your project team, you need to:

1. Recognize sources of team dissension
2. Become attuned to indicators of poor morale
3. Understand the characteristics of an effective team
4. Know how to build esprit de corps
5. Breed commitment and accountability among employees
6. Understand your impact on team performance
7. Improve the physical work environment

Sources of team dissension

Every team has the potential for dissension, even anarchy, as well as extreme conformity. Many sources for this dissension exist.

One common source of dissension is having no leaders

Project Manager
Senior Management
Client
Programmer
Configuration Management Specialist
Program Planner
Quality Assurance Specialist
Analyst
Finance Specialist
Integration Specialist
Architect
Auditor
Training Specialist
Engineer
Technical Writer
Industrial Engineer
Purchasing Specialist
Legal Specialist
Material Specialist
Facilities Specialist
Hardware Specialist
Laboratory Environment Specialist
Suppliers
Subcontractors
Implementation Specialist
Maintenance Specialist

Figure 12.1   *Some specialized roles involved in a typical project*

appointed for the project. If more than ten people are assigned
to your team and you appoint no leaders, the likelihood of
factions forming in your group increases. Informal leaders
may arise, each competing for dominance.

Quite often a feeling exists among professionals that leadership is unnecessary, that it inhibits people's performance.
After all, they think, we are all professionals and we will
perform accordingly.

Such thoughts are fallacious. Because of the specialized
roles participants have in projects, leadership is essential (see
Figure 12.1). A strong need arises for someone to facilitate,
coordinate, communicate, and allocate to ensure that everything comes together to produce a final product. When such
leadership is absent, projects resemble a group of blind skiers

crashing into one another; only a few of them reach the bottom of the hill in one piece. Or imagine the sound of a one hundred piece orchestra without a conductor. The component parts are assembled, but the necessary leadership is missing.

The misallocation of resources is another source of team dissension. A situation where people receive equipment who have no need for it while those who do need it go without can cause frustration, jealousy, and anger. And that can threaten to tear the team apart.

Microcomputers are a prime example of this. Some team members have a microcomputer on their desk and others do not. What is interesting is that some of the people who have a machine never use it but keep it as a status symbol. Others who need to use a microcomputer fight over the machine that they must share. Having these people perform their tasks without a microcomputer can prove more costly and counterproductive to the project. All this could be resolved by reallocating the microcomputer to those people who need it based upon the tasks that they must perform.

Mistrust also threatens team unity. People sometimes spread vicious rumours about another person. Or people are afraid to initiate any task for fear of criticism, even ostracism, by their peers. Anger and resentment foment which can result in a win–lose atmosphere.

When a project appears to be failing, this breeds an atmosphere of mistrust. Everyone starts protecting their turf and arming themselves for the day when someone points the finger at them. Programmers, for example, blame the systems analysts for not developing accurate specifications. Systems analysts blame the programmers for deviating from the specifications. Data analysts and technical writers claim that they received no cooperation from either the programmers or the systems analysts.

Insufficient resources will destroy team unity, too. Some people will swindle or cheat to acquire what they consider to be their fair share of supplies. Some team members will feel angry about why some people received ample resources and they received little or none.

Another source of dissension is poor unity of command where people work for more than one person. A project in a matrix environment can be especially hazardous. In a matrix environment, the team member reports to the project manager and the functional manager, thereby serving two bosses. Sometimes a conflict results. The employee finds himself torn between supporting the project manager or the functional manager. This conflict can tear the team apart with some members favouring the project manager and others backing their functional manager.

When team members working in a matrix environment know a speciality that no colleague knows, they may have to support several different projects. The stress becomes even more acute when they must support two or more projects that must meet deadlines around the same time. Unless they can resolve this difficulty, they will face conflict with their functional managers, the project managers, and their fellow team members.

Inadequate span of control can contribute to disunity. If your team is too large, exceeding more than ten people, and you have not designated a leader, your control of the group will become difficult. That is because you have exceeded the maximum number of people over whom you can have effective control. When your team becomes larger than ten people, appoint leaders to eliminate the opportunity for the team to break into factions.

Favouritism by senior management towards a particular team member will also contribute to disunity. A team member may have, for instance, 'connections' and consequently, will affect the way others behave towards you and the project.

Favouritism on your part towards an individual can also lead to disunity. Too close an association with a team member can lead to accusations of favouritism and make your judgements appear less than objective. Such circumstances can lead to an 'us' versus 'them' syndrome, the 'us' being you and your favourites and the 'them' being the team members who feel neglected.

Lack of clear direction will lead to disunity, especially for projects involving highly specialized disciplines. People may do their work well but each one goes in a different direction because no one told or reminded them of the goals and objectives of the project. Their performance resembles a bag of water falling on the floor and breaking, with the liquid spraying in all directions.

That occurs especially on some projects where requirements have not been defined. Team members begin doing their own thing after the project manager tells them to start working while he goes to the client to determine what is required. By the time the project manager returns, team members have gone in different directions.

Poor role definition can also cause disunity. People have little or no idea of what they are to do, or are doing, on the project. If they start work, they could be doing something that someone else is already doing. That can result in disagreements, even disputes, over responsibilities.

This can arise on highly specialized projects if tasks and their assignments have not been defined clearly. Team members start replicating tasks. This can result in re-work, confusion, frustration, and lower productivity which, in turn, means schedule slides, budget overruns, and poor workmanship.

Finally, poor or no resource levelling can cause serious disunity. A common example of this is where a few productive individuals are relied on to compensate for the mediocre performance of the other team members. The project manager gives the best assignments to these few individuals while the others handle the less challenging ones and have no opportunity to become outstanding team members. This can lead to jealousy on the part of both the exceptional and the mediocre. The former feel that the project manager is overworking and taking advantage of them; the latter feel that the project manager has favourites and is not providing opportunities for everyone.

Maintaining team unity is critical for a successful project. People on the project must work together as a cohesive unit. That does not mean absolute conformity but does mean that you must establish a cooperative atmosphere, otherwise, you will be managing only conflicts rather than the entire project.

Indicators of poor morale

Some project managers behave like an ostrich with its head in the sand. They fail to look for cues that tell them that something is wrong. This is especially the case when dealing with their project team. The main reason for this oversight is that project managers tend to be task-oriented rather than people-oriented. They focus on what must be done. Yet to complete the project they must work through people. Without the co-operation of team members, the project manager will fail. As a project manager, therefore, you should constantly be alert to indicators of poor morale. Taken by itself, one incident involving a morale indicator should not alarm you. But intensified reoccurrences should.

Several indicators reveal poor morale. Some common ones are:

- argumentative sessions at meetings
- low productivity
- poor quality of workmanship
- outright refusal to perform
- insubordination
- excessive absenteeism
- high turnover
- power struggles (factioning)
- spread of negative rumors
- sabotage of other people's work

When a serious morale problem does arise, you cannot ignore it because it will get worse. You must address the problem as early as possible by identifying the root cause and fixing it.

The best approach is to have a confidential discussion with the parties involved and try to resolve the problem. Communicate that such behaviour is not acceptable and that the consequences of their actions do no one any good, especially the project. Strive for positive resolution rather than resorting to negative measures, such as formal warnings or firing people (if you have that power). Whatever approach you take, however, is better than not taking one at all.

Characteristics of high morale

Good project managers know the difference between teams with esprit de corps and those continually plagued with morale problems. They do whatever is necessary to ensure their teams have these characteristics of high morale:

- little or no dissension
- mutual trust among members
- well-defined and understood goals and objectives
- high esprit de corps
- well-defined roles and responsibilities
- good communication up and down the chain of command
- assigned backups for each other's tasks
- appointed leadership
- equitable distribution of resources

These are only a few characteristics of teams with high morale, but they are nonetheless very important. Such teams arise not by circumstance but by design. The project manager lays the groundwork for teams with esprit de corps.

High esprit de corps

Building high morale among team members is not easy. People vary in their backgrounds and consequently view reality differently. Their perceptions of you and the project will vary, thereby making it difficult to maintain team unity. Ways exist, however, to build that esprit de corps.

First, you need to communicate clearly to the team its goals and objectives. Everyone on your team should know the mission. While sounding like common sense, that may not necessarily happen on a large project using many people with specialized skills. Quite often, if the project manager fails to focus people's attention on the overall goal, people will tend to go their separate ways. The consequence is much work but ineffective.

An excellent way to communicate to team members the goal of the project is to give them a mission statement. This statement, typically the first or second paragraphs of the statement of work, should capture what the project must accomplish. Team members can then perform their work while always reminding themselves of the question, 'Is what I am doing and how I am doing it contributing to the success of the project?' If the answer is negative, they can adjust their mode of operation accordingly.

Let everyone know how important their contribution is to your project. Clarify the role each person plays in completing the mission. Team members sometimes fail to see the total picture and consequently do not understand, or care about the impact of their actions.

Due to the various specialists involved in a technical project, many team members fail to understand the impact of their work on others. Many focus only on their responsibilities not realizing that their delays or poor workmanship affects the performance of those receiving the output. In addition, they lack an understanding of the entire project life cycle.

A good technique is to show team members the complete network diagram, pinpointing the dependencies of each task and who is responsible for completing each one. The best approach is to hold a group meeting to review the network diagram and explain the interdependencies between the tasks.

Hold joint meetings; that is, hold meetings with everyone on the team present. Infrequent meetings between two or three members (if the team is much larger) can break the team into factions. You should hold such meetings regularly so members have a sense of community and the opportunity to communicate with one another. Staff meetings are an effective means for creating esprit de corps, if conducted correctly. These meetings are usually held weekly, often in the early part of the week. Although as project manager you run the meeting, you allow people to participate by sharing experiences and providing solutions to common problems.

Try to provide people with the opportunity for growth. Some project managers give key assignments to select individuals which sometimes backfires because other team members feel neglected and their motivation declines. Jealousy often arises, leading to mediocrity in some and exceptional performance in others. The best approach is to give everyone the opportunity to excel, not just a few people.

For instance, avoid the tendency of having 'pet' team members. That occurs frequently because the project manager relies on one individual due to expertise or personality. Such reliance breeds jealousy and makes the project manager dependent on one person.

Avoid doing everything yourself. Delegate some tasks and do not delegate to just a few individuals. One popular way to delegate is to rotate the opportunity for people to act as the project manager during your absence. If you are away for any length of time, for example at a seminar or on vacation, give everyone on the team the chance to play the project manager. This gives people the opportunity to grow and allows you to identify who would be excellent candidates for your replacement.

Be a good listener rather than just a good talker. Telling rather than listening widens the communication gap and leads to hearing only what you want to hear, not what you need to hear. Failure to listen to opposing arguments, for example, will break the team into two camps; those supporting what you want to hear and those disagreeing silently. That is a sure prescription for destroying team unity.

Make sure that good formal communications have been established. Hold review sessions and staff meetings; give people copies of the project handbook and procedures; allow for open-door sessions; and have responsibility matrices and schedules in place. The best rule is that if something has the potential for improving communications then use it.

A simple, effective way to ensure good communications is to develop and distribute a documentation matrix similar to the one shown in Figure 12.2. In the left column are listed all the major participants in the project. The top row lists the various documents. Where they intersect indicates who should receive a copy of the documentation. The advantage of the matrix is that it helps ensure people receive the documentation

TOPICS \ NAMES	SAFETY HANDBOOK	FINANCE POLICIES	SECURITY HANDBOOK	TOOL ORDERING HANDBOOK	EQUIPMENT REPAIR HANDBOOK	CODE AND ETHICS HANDBOOK
SMITH	X			X	X	X
JONES						X
WEBSTER			X		X	X
COCHRAN				X		X
GEBHARDT		X				X
WILLIAMS					X	X

Figure 12.2   *Documentation matrix*

they need, keeping them up-to-date with what is occurring on the project. This advantage is increased if you include the matrix in the project handbook.

Encourage opportunities for people to work jointly on a task. Sharing responsibilities gives people the chance to communicate with each other and not feel alone. It also gives team members the opportunity to learn from others new methods and techniques.

Some computing companies segregate roles on a project team. Systems analysts may work independently of systems designers, who work independently of programmers, and the programmers work independently of technical writers and everyone else. They communicate only via documentation. This has hazards, and does not offer people the opportunity to learn about each other's work and role in the project. As a result there is a danger of poor communication and less teamwork. The best approach is to encourage a multi-disciplinary approach to completing a task.

The key to building esprit de corps is to see each team member as a part in an intricately constructed whole – like a watch. All the parts, no matter how insignificant, must work

- Cordinate effort of selected people having different perspectives/opinions
- Unify and integrate people's knowledge and experience base
- Direct attention to specific topics
- Document findings
- Use team approach to obtain commitment and encourage good team dynamics
- Address people side as well as hardside issues
- Reduce flowtime for decision-making
- Address communication and coordination
- Use brainstorming and other problem-solving techniques
- Track and monitor progress after a decision has been made

Figure 12.3 *Guidelines for participative management*

together if the watch is to function. If any part fails to function, you must repair the watch.

Commitment and accountability

Some project managers start without assigning responsibilities. The team functions like a mass of jelly without form or substance. Accountability brings structure to your project; you can inculcate structure accountability in many ways.

One way is to encourage signatures on all significant documents. Signing documents forces people to review work for accuracy and encourages people to comply with the contents. You should encourage signatures on documents like the network diagram, work breakdown structures, minutes of meetings, reports, and action lists. You should also obtain signatures on technical documents. A person cannot help but comply with the contents of a document that they have signed; otherwise, their credibility declines.

Another method is to use participative management (see Figure 12.3). People participating in decision-making are less likely to criticize the decision. Even if they do not agree with the ultimate decision, they tend not to object because they have had their say. Still another effective method is by delegating tasks. This breeds commitment and accountability among employees. Like participative management, employees who receive delegated tasks become participants in the decision-making process, and are thereby less likely to criticize the results.

You can also recognize employees who have performed exceedingly well on your project. By giving visibility to a team member's performance, you encourage that person's emotional commitment to the project. The more a person identifies with a project the harder it is for them to disassociate themselves from it.

Inviting the right people to meetings makes sense yet often does not happen. Knowing who to invite to a meeting is almost as important as having the meeting. Often, people attend a meeting without having any idea of its purpose. The result is lost productive time and a perplexed team member. After making sure the right people attend your meeting, you should have minutes taken, approved, and distributed among all participants.

Finally, use the power of the memo to breed commitment and accountability (see Figure 12.4). Whenever you hold a meeting with someone, especially with a customer, draft a memo of understanding detailing the result and circulate it. People will then hesitate to renege on their agreements.

Your impact on team performance

No one has greater impact on team performance than you. How you lead your team can affect the outcome of the project. You send the signals that people will respond to, and unless you send the right signals, there may be serious problems.

Establishing a positive work environment gives one signal you want to send. Removing obstacles to their performance and providing open communications up and down the chain of command let people know that you want a successful project.

- Identifies:
    - Distribution list
    - Originator
    - Creation date
    - Subject
- Clear
- Concise
- Well-organized
- Typed
- Signed

Figure 12.4   *Characteristics of a good memo*

Also, look for opportunities to maximize people's strengths rather than harping on their weaknesses.

Setting an example provides another signal that you want to send. Follow the standards that you establish for your team. Do not criticize or blame people for doing the same things that you have done.

Displaying your vision, too, is necessary. Many project managers wander about aimlessly without any real idea of what they must do. If they do not know, how can they expect the team members to know? These project managers are typically indecisive because they lack any sense of direction for the project. If you do not know exactly where the project is heading, you will communicate your lack of confidence and team members will lose confidence in you.

Finally, display trust in yourself and your team. If you ever violate that trust, you sacrifice your credibility, and once that occurs, managing the project becomes very difficult. People will not believe in you. You then become the biggest liability to the project.

The physical work environment

The physical working environment can have a big impact on the productivity of your team. Poor facilities and inadequate equipment can make even routine tasks a chore.

The number of physical conditions that negatively affect the productivity of a project are countless. The following lists a few:

- crowded desks
- constantly ringing telephones
- insufficient number of photocopiers
- poor lighting
- antiquated equipment
- unreliable equipment
- air too cold, hot, or humid
- heavy pedestrian traffic
- excessive noise
- inadequate facilities (e.g., no cafeteria or bathrooms)
- insufficient supplies

- poorly designed equipment
- depressing wall colouring
- lack of windows

These problems, and many others, will have a negative impact on productivity. Although you may be unable to change many of them, you can take some steps to alleviate their effect.

If people must constantly fight to use equipment such as a microcomputer, you can establish a schedule to regulate its use. For instance, one person can use it from 8am to 10am and another from 1pm to 3pm. Or you can place a sheet next to the equipment for people to indicate the time that they will need the machine. You might consider restricting the length of time that a person can use the equipment, e.g. no more than a block of two hours at a time.

If limited supplies exist, you can ration or purchase limited quantities and then establish priority usage. If the work area appears dismal, people can bring personal items to the office to improve its appearance. Plants and pictures are common fixtures brought to workstations. These items should be 'tasteful' and not interfere with completion of the project.

You should do whatever is in your power to provide a comfortable working environment. A good question to ask yourself is: If I were that team member, what in the environment would negatively affect my productivity? If you list anything, then you have a clue that you should fix something. Perhaps the team member is already aware of the problem but was afraid to mention it. Or perhaps everyone on the team is shy about telling you a problem. Both circumstances serve as clues that something is having a negative effect on productivity and that you should take necessary action.

Effective teambuilding

A project team is more than the sum of its parts. To work effectively and efficiently you need to provide the leadership and environment that encourages everyone to participate as an integral part of your project.

Chapter 13

Dealing with the client

Project managers need to cooperate closely with the people for whom the product is being built. Without that cooperation, managing the people side of project management can prove very difficult.

The best way to engender that cooperation is to understand what should be expected from both parties so that managing the people side of project management will have positive results.

Expectations of the project manager

The project manager has a set of expectations of the client. These include expectations of the client's role in the project and the type of actions that will be involved. The client, therefore, is expected to:

- Communicate requirements
- Understand the work of the project team
- Avoid stereotyping
- Not indulge in scapegoating
- Provide time and resources
- Designate focal points
- Attend meetings
- Be willing to experiment
- Take ownership

153

Communicate requirements

Project managers expect their clients to communicate requirements. This is the cornerstone for building a meaningful product. Yet many clients fail to provide the time and/or people to define requirements. And even if they do, they provide such support at a minimal level.

Without that support project managers can employ all the tools and techniques available for capturing requirements, such as models or prototypes, and still fail to capture the requirements adequately.

Clients who show a willingness to communicate requirements will designate people to provide partial or full-time support to the project. Other ways of demonstrating support include providing time and money to capture requirements as well as sending representatives to meetings.

Understanding the work

Although many clients want the project manager and their team to have an understanding of their environment, they often fail to express a reciprocal interest. Yet such an understanding is necessary for participation in the project's life cycle.

Project managers should expect the client to understand the rudimentary tasks of building the product. Some firms solve that problem by placing team members with the client. These team members have the responsibility for communicating requirements and the necessary background to communicate with other project teams.

Avoid stereotyping

People have the tendency to simplify in order to deal with the complexities of the working world. Having preconceived notions is one way to do this.

Many clients harbour images of technical professionals which can make managing a project difficult and they may have these images even before meeting a team member. Some common images include viewing team members as having no interest in the client's requirements, being poor communicators, and wanting only to play with high-tech toys. Project managers must work to overcome such preconceived notions. They can do this by ensuring client representatives and team members work in the same environment, attend meetings together, and by encouraging as many joint reviews as possible. Such closeness cannot help but encourage greater communication and understanding between team members and the client.

No scapegoating

People tend to blame other people for their problems and when this is prevalent, it can make managing a project very difficult.

The project team, for example, might blame the client for not cooperating. The client, however, may blame the project team, even the project manager, for problems when they alone may be responsible.

The ways a client can shift the blame are endless. These include accusing team members of having poor communication skills and no interest in their side of business. While sometimes true, these accusations are frequently a cover for the poor performance and lack of cooperation on the client's side. This type of scapegoating results in damaged communication and destroyed trust among all project participants.

Project managers can help prevent scapegoating by identifying sources of problems quickly. They do that by identifying and eliminating causes rather than addressing symptoms.

They can also take further action. They can ensure continued interaction between project team members and the client. Whenever a problem arises, they should encourage both parties to work jointly to share the responsibility and determine a solution.

Time and resources

Perhaps one of the biggest signs of client interest in a project is the time and resources it allocates to the endeavour. Very little interest manifests itself through minimal contribution of time and resources, such as people or money or both. The opposite indicates a greater interest in the project.

The following scenario occurs on many projects. The client emphasizes how important the project is to its current and future operations and, therefore, wants the project. As time passes, however, the client either finds its needs or priorities changing or it simply provides minimum support. Gradually, support fades as representatives from the client attend fewer meetings, resist increases in budget, or provide little time for participating in any phase of the project life cycle. A decline in providing time and resources becomes the norm rather than the exception.

Project managers must deal with this if they hope to deliver a product. Some useful people side approaches include documenting the impact of a decline of support on schedules; recording the client's lack of presence at meetings in the minutes; preparing periodic status reports detailing the impact of limited time and resources; and, keeping the avenue of communications between all parties open, such as requiring decisions by the client at periodic points throughout the project life cycle.

Designate focal points

In large organizations, 'the client' may really signify a substantial number of people. Under such circumstances, dealing with the client can prove cumbersome and difficult.

To make things easier, the client should provide a list of focal points: liaison people that team members can consult regarding particular topics. It neither benefits the client nor the team if project members must spend excess time looking for answers or agreements. Of course, the client should select as focal points people who have an understanding of computing and good interpersonal skills.

Attend meetings

A concomitant of devoting time and resources is for the client to have attendees at significant meetings. Their presence is necessary to discuss and define requirements, resolve disagreements, and communicate information. However, that can only happen if the client and the attendees have an interest in the meetings and not just a presence.

Project managers should have representatives of the client at several meetings, including status review, checkpoint review, and authorization meetings. They should solicit the participation of the representatives and even encourage them to make decisions.

Willingness to experiment

Project managers should expect the client to allow the project team to try different approaches to meet requirements and specifications.

Many clients prefer to pursue paths that are efficient and effective which often entails building products the way they have been done for years. While familiarity is helpful, it can also lead to the repetition of mistakes. Circumstances change and few projects are the same because often too many variables exist. The client needs to understand that.

Many clients are comfortable (though not necessarily happy) with following the traditional life cycle where each phase in a project occurs sequentially. Yet other life cycles exist (for example, as in data processing) which could help expedite and even improve project performance and product. Many techniques also exist for developing products; however, some clients do not want to experiment with those techniques because they do not want to become the guinea pigs.

Project managers must make the effort to encourage the client to experiment. They can accomplish that by explaining the benefits of experimenting with a different life cycle or technique, citing statistics and examples as well as providing demonstrations. They can also provide a comparative analysis and review of the traditional way versus the new way. They must be willing to prove the need to experiment rather than simply expect acquiescence from the client.

Take ownership

Above all, project managers should expect clients to take ownership of the system. That means that the client should feel that the product is theirs when being developed, and when delivered – not the project manager's.

This makes sense because the clients are the ones paying for the product, not the project managers. Taking ownership requires, however, that clients show an interest in their projects early. This interest involves taking an active part in planning, participating in, and administering projects.

Project managers can encourage ownership in many ways. They can invite clients to all meetings, even technical ones, request from the clients input and feedback during all critical moments of the project, and keep clients informed of the status of the project. The important point is that clients must feel that the product is theirs, not something 'dumped in their laps'.

Expectations of the client

Clients have certain expectations about the role of project managers. These expectations affect how well the people side of project management will proceed and, consequently, how well projects will accomplish their goals and objectives. These expectations about project managers include:

- Being honest
- Knowing the business
- Having technical expertise
- Keeping current
- Being cooperative
- Communicating
- Providing the best output

Being honest

Lose credibility with clients and project managers lose their ability to interact with them. Communications will come to a standstill and the future will appear dismal. Clients expect project managers to plan and report honestly. That means providing honest input and feedback regarding schedules, budgets, and quality. Clients do not want 'guessing games' or 'hidden agendas'; they expect the facts, even if they might not want to hear the facts.

To ensure honesty and, consequently, credibility, project managers should invite clients to attend meetings and even work sessions. In addition, they should brief clients regularly regarding the status of the budget, schedule, and quality. These actions will make clients feel that project managers are straightforward and honest.

Knowing the business

Clients also expect project managers and teams to take a sincere interest in their business's functions and interactions. That means learning and capturing all the who, what, when, where, why, and how information needed to build a product. Clients do not want to simply hand out money, leave the computing professionals to do the work and then receive a product that upsets the entire work environment. They want a product that they can integrate into their work environment rather than have to change the way of doing business to meet the needs of the product.

Project managers can express an interest in the business considerations of their clients in several ways. They can appoint team members whose primary tasks are to capture requirements, have team members who reside in the clients' workplaces, and always address the client's concerns at all meetings.

Having technical expertise

Clients expect technical expertise, not so much from the project managers but from the project teams. They want the best for their money and do not want to pay for the mistakes and learning curve of others. Failure to exude an image of technical expertise can affect other expectations, including credibility.

Project managers can satisfy this expectation in many ways. One way is to provide the client with copies of the team members' C.V.s. Another is to appoint specific members on the team (the ones with the most talent, experience, and knowledge) to liaise with the client. Finally, project managers can have team members review technical output as an effort to show that team members possess the requisite expertise to perform well.

Keeping current

Keeping current is a necessity but clients expect that of their project managers in all areas of their projects. This includes knowing the latest on the schedule, budget, and technical performance. Possessing such knowledge reassures clients that project managers are 'on top of the situation'.

Project managers can employ several measures to assure their client that they are keeping abreast. They can conduct ad hoc and regularly scheduled meetings with the client present; provide periodic status update briefings; and, give the client documents reflecting the status on schedule, budget, and technical performance.

Being cooperative

To succeed, projects require the cooperation of all participants. Perhaps the cooperation which is most important is that between the client and the project manager and his team. If that relationship deteriorates, the people side of project management becomes complicated.

Project managers must show that they and their team members seek that cooperation as much as the client does. They can do that by showing a sincere interest in the business aspects of the project by matching technical sophistication to the requirements of the client, and by showing an appreciation for the client's need to address operational needs as well as technical ones.

Communicating

Closely aligned to cooperation is communication. Clients expect project managers to communicate with them, but that communication involves more than just speaking. It entails communicating in a way that the client will understand, in other words, without resorting to jargon.

The technical professional uses many esoteric terms and concepts. Project managers must translate these terms and concepts so that the client does not feel overwhelmed and even defensive.

Project managers can communicate with the client in several ways. They can provide training for the clients; short sessions can explain the technical objectives, problems, and concerns of the project. They can hold ad hoc and regularly scheduled meetings. Finally, they can encourage the client to review all documentation for feedback, not necessarily approval.

Providing the best output

Above all, clients expect to receive the most for their money. They want the best output regarding schedule, budget, and product.

When expectations become unrealistic, project managers must correct them at an early stage. They can do this by presenting a realistic portrait of the practicality of the project, such as the risks, the capabilities of the team, the constraints, and limitations facing the project.

Armed with such information, project managers can bring all parties down to earth and eliminate unrealistic expectations.

Working together

Both project manager and client have expectations about how each should perform. How well both parties meet those expectations will affect how well the project meets its goals and objectives. Project managers must recognize the reality of those expectations if they hope to manage the people side of project management.

Chapter 14

Dealing with senior management

Project managers must deal with a number of audiences if they expect to complete their projects on time and within budget. Quite often, most discussion is about their relationships with the client and the project team. Yet, project managers must deal with another party that can dramatically influence the outcome of their projects: senior management.

The role of senior management

Senior management play an instrumental role in the planning and implementation of a project. During the planning, they must establish the parameters of the project. That is, they must help formulate the goals and objectives of the project and decide on the level of support required to accomplish them. Their decisions will partly reflect the need to meet those of the client but will also fall within their own strategic plans and policies. In sum, they set the direction for the project.

During the implementation of a project, senior management monitor progress at a high level. They review summary information on schedule, budget, and quality to ensure that the project meets the client's needs and their expectations.

Counter-productive actions of senior management

During the planning and implementation of a project, senior management can take counter-productive actions that can influence the outcome of a project. Senior management may start 'micromanaging' a project by handling the project's daily major and minor activities; by contradicting or usurping the authority of the project manager; and by managing the affairs of project team members.

Senior management may also succumb to pressure from the client for fear of losing current and future business. They may, consequently, allow the client to dictate the management of the project, including the technical aspects. Whatever the client wants is permitted. The result is a demoralized project team and project manager who find themselves losing the professional autonomy to do their work.

Some senior managers try to sabotage a project. They may not have favoured the project from the start. They may feel that the project is not fulfilling their concept of the strategic plans or is competing with their 'pet' projects for scarce resources.

Other senior managers try to sabotage a project for fear of being upstaged. They see the project manager becoming a rising star who could jeopardize their position. A project manager of a large project can receive considerable visibility and experience that prepares them for higher positions – senior management positions, specifically their positions. Hence, the need to sabotage the project.

Expectations from senior management

To a large degree, these counter-productive actions of senior management are due to certain expectations that they have of the project manager. When these expectations are unfulfilled, senior management become nervous. It is important that project managers know these expectations, which are:

- Being honest
- Taking decisive action
- Possessing expertise

- Doing a good job
- Commitment to project
- Communicating

Being honest

Being honest and straightforward is one expectation. Senior management want project managers to report not only what they want to hear but need to hear. In other words, they expect project managers to report negative as well as positive information. They do not want project managers to keep them 'in the dark' until it is too late.

Taking decisive action

Having the ability to take decisive action is another expectation. They expect project managers to make decisions when required, without first having to ask for permission. Senior management do not and should not manage the daily affairs of projects.

Possessing expertise

Senior management want project managers to have some expertise about the subject of their projects. That is not the same as being an expert because being one can have a negative affect on managing the project. Rather, senior management expect project managers to know enough about the subject to keep abreast of the progress of the project and be able to communicate with the client and team members.

Doing a good job

Desiring to do a good job and not being an empire builder is another expectation of senior management. They want project managers who concentrate on getting the job done and not enlarging their fiefdom. They place people in a position of trust and expect them to use that position to complete their projects on time, within budget, and to the highest quality.

Commitment to project

Closely allied to the last expectation is that senior management want project managers committed to the success of their projects. They expect project managers to remain for the entire duration of the project rather than defect as soon as their projects run into trouble.

Communicating

Finally, senior management expect project managers to inform them about the status of their projects. They expect regular reports on schedule, budget, and quality. They also expect those reports to be in a form that they can relate to. They do not want to wade through a mass of technical and micromanagement details, but instead want meaningful summary information.

Project managers' expectations of senior management

Project managers, too, have expectations about senior management. These expectations include:

- Guidance and direction
- Autonomy
- Support
- Commitment

Guidance and direction

They expect guidance and direction from senior management. Project managers, for instance, should know what the organization's strategy is regarding systems development. They can then plan, organize, and conduct their projects incorporating that strategy. If senior management fail to provide a strategy, however, project managers will operate under a cloud of uncertainty without having any assurance that their projects will continue.

Autonomy

Project managers expect autonomy in managing their projects. They do not expect or want senior management to make every decision and intervene in the daily affairs of their projects. Any suggestion of micromanagement will generate adverse feeling on their part and on the part of team members.

Support

They also expect support from senior management. Project managers expect financial support but something else that senior management often overlook – political support. They want senior management to give visibility to their projects by expressing support in many ways, such as talking about their projects at meetings and taking a bona fide interest in the progress of their projects.

Commitment

Closely allied to the last expectation is the one that senior management should commit themselves to the outcome of their projects. This commitment is both private and public and should remain even when the project heads towards disaster. Senior management sometimes do not hesitate to cut their commitment to projects that appear to be heading for trouble. Under such circumstances, project managers feel that they and their team have been abandoned.

Meeting both expectations

Because you are the one who must handle the fate of your projects, you must undertake several actions to ensure a positive relationship exists with senior management. First, you can encourage senior management to review and approve the project plan. By encouraging senior management's participation, you will at least implicitly commit them to your projects. If senior management do not want to review and approve your project plan, it implies that your project is not on their priority list.

You can provide regular updates for senior management. Such reviews keep them informed of your project's progress. This has another benefit. The review keeps your project in the foreground. In other words, it lends visibility to your project.

You can also provide the right information to senior management by presenting only information that they need to know and in summary form. Presenting irrelevant and detailed information not only irritates senior management but also encourages them to micromanage.

You should obtain a project sponsor. This could be one or more members of senior management who openly embrace your project and lobby for support. Having the right allies in senior management can increase the visibility of your project. Without a sponsor, you will find yourself immersed in the politics of senior management and could find your project short-lived due to a loss of importance relative to other projects.

You can also become politically attuned to what is happening in senior management. Although you may not be a senior manager, you depend on their good graces and, therefore, you need to think in their terms if you hope to ensure continued support for your project. Being simply a follower of orders and a technical expert is not enough. This does not mean, however, trying to be involved in the politics of senior management. It means that you must know what is happening.

Finally, you can continually remind senior management of your project not only to fulfil their strategic visions for the organization but also for the entire company. If you can convince senior management of the importance of your project, you can expect political endorsement as well as fiscal support.

Working together

As a project manager you must deal with a wide range of people, including senior management. You must handle your relationship with senior management with as much skill as you do with the project team and the client. Without having the support of senior management, you will find managing projects very difficult, even impossible.

Epilogue

To manage a project successfully, project managers need an appropriate blend of skills. These skills can be divided into two categories, 'hard' and 'soft'. Ideally, a project manager should have a mixture of both hard and soft skills.

Hard skills

Hard skills are ones that project managers acquire through training and experience.

Good product knowledge is one hard skill. They should know something about the product being built. If the product is an autopilot system, they should know about software and aerodynamics. If their product is a complex building, they should know about construction.

Notice that the word 'good' precedes product knowledge. Effective project managers do not need to be the most technically superior. Indeed, sometimes people with the most knowledge about technology do not make the best project managers. Some people, though highly proficient technically, may lack the skills required to manage projects effectively.

For instance, being the best mechanical or electrical engineer does not qualify a person to become a project manager nor does being the best technical writer or draughtsman. He or she may have expertise in only one area and may lack the skills, knowledge, and experience in other important areas that are critical for being an effective project manager.

Ironically, often these people are promoted precisely because of their technical expertise. Once they become project managers, they find themselves fulfilling the Peter Principle. They have been promoted to their level of incompetence because they lack the other skills required for success as a project manager.

Engineers, for instance, are notorious for being technically proficient but disastrous as project managers, although exceptions do exist. Frequently, however, engineers take charge of projects while they lack other important skills. Many of them lack these skills simply as a result of previous experience or having graduated without taking courses in soft skills.

Good product knowledge is important but insufficient. Project managers must also have a solid understanding of statistics and maths. They must work with figures to determine past performance and what the future will be. That requires the use of charts, illustrations, curves, and reports with numerical data to make well-informed decisions.

In addition, project managers need to have excellent planning skills. They must methodically develop well-defined goals and specific objectives, determining the steps required to complete their projects, in what order, and when. Furthermore, they must be able to estimate the requirements for completing a task and an entire project.

Project managers also need to have good writing skills. They must know how to draft clear, concise documentation that will improve rather than confuse activities (see Figure E.1). They must know which documents to write, their appropriate format, and when to prepare them. Specifically, they must know how to prepare memos, status reports, correspondence with clients, project procedures, and other project documentation.

They must also have good public speaking skills (see Figure E.2). Because they often attend and give presentations, they must be able to communicate information about their product. That requires having the ability to converse with many people, from technicians to generalists. Project managers must

- Has title
- Signatures and date
- Clear
- Concise
- Readable
- Complete
- Concrete language
- Organization
- Continuity
- Logical flow
- Consistent
- Uniform
- Modifications and updates separately identified
- Version controlled
- Abstract
- Table of contents
- Glossary
- Index
- Acronyms list
- Illustrations
- Good spelling and punctuation

Figure E.1   *Qualities of good documentation*

communicate to various people on the project team, their management, and with the client.

Soft skills

Project managers will not succeed if they have only the necessary hard skills. They also need the appropriate 'soft' skills. These skills are termed soft because project managers can learn about them but still require considerable experience in their application before mastering them. Almost anyone, for instance, can learn descriptive statistics but not everyone can be an effective listener quickly.

That is a necessary soft skill for project managers (see Figure E.3). They must discern what is significant and what is not at meetings and during conversations while not necessarily agreeing with what was said either by the client, senior management, or project team members. For example, senior programmers, programmer analysts, and systems analysts must have effective listening skills since they must interact

DELIVERY	MATERIAL	PREPARATION
AUDIENCE INVOLVEMENT	ORGANIZATION	AUDIENCE ASSESSMENT
EYE CONTACT	VISUALS	AGENDA
VOICE PROJECTION	CONCLUSION	PURPOSE
BODY LANGUAGE	CLOSING AND WRAP-UP	HANDOUTS
QUESTION AND ANSWER PERIOD	OPENING STATEMENT	LOCATION
DURATION	IDENTIFY KEY POINTS	
EQUIPMENT USAGE	SPELLING/PUNCTUATION	
MAINTAIN INTEREST	COMPLETE	
MAINTAIN CONTROL	CONSISTENT	
ENTHUSIASM	UNIFORM	
LANGUAGE	LOGICAL FLOW	
CREDIBILITY	READABLE (LARGE TYPE)	
CONFIDENCE	AVOID CLUTTER	
GOOD LISTENER	RESTRICT NUMBER OF LINES PER PAGE	
INFLUENCE AUDIENCE ATTITUDE	RESTRICT NUMBER OF WORDS PER PAGE	
ENCOURAGE FEEDBACK	IMPLEMENTATION SPECIALIST	
	MAINTENANCE SPECIALIST	

Figure E.2 *Checklist for effective presentations*

- Maintains eye contact
- Communicates verbally
- Communicates non-verbally
- Appears attentive, alert, interested, and involved
- Encourages talking through use of questions
- Provides recognition and constructive feedback
- Focuses attention on talker
- Listens to understand
- Does not dominate the conversation

Figure E.3 *Characteristics of an effective listener*

- Agenda used and followed
- Everyone has a chance to speak
- No one dominates
- Chairperson conducts, but does not overcontrol
- All relevant persons present
- Minutes are recorded
- Irrelevant topics not addressed
- Large enough room used
- Adequate supplies and equipment available
- Comfortable environmental conditions exist

Figure E.4 *Guidelines for conducting an effective meeting*

with the client, capture requirements, and obtain feedback. Yet so many times the client claims that the system it received 'does not give us what we wanted' or, 'that's not what we asked for'. Lack of effective listening skills contributes to this problem and if one of those individuals becomes project manager, the relationship with team members, the client, and senior management will suffer.

Successful project managers do not 'screen' out what they do not want to hear. Some project managers only want to hear positive feedback and pretend that negative information does not exist. Others pay attention only to the negative. Either way, both types are poor listeners and perform like an 'ostrich with its head in the sand'.

Running effective meetings is another soft skill project managers must have (see Figure E.4). They not only attend meetings, they also run them. To have productive meetings,

- Act now; avoid procrastination
- Plan, allocate, and prioritize your time
- Create and maintain a time log
- Delegate tasks when appropriate
- Challenge yourself with positive stress
- Create to-do lists
- Categorize work as urgent, important, busy or file
- Provide and expect clear communication
- Make time available for uninterrupted concentration
- Leave some personal 'free' time for yourself
- Use time effectively first; rank efficiency second
- Define your goals and objectives
- Say 'no' when necessary

Figure E.5   *Guidelines for effective time management*

they know that just holding them is not enough. They must provide leadership by addressing the important issues efficiently and effectively. That entails having meaningful meetings, not just sessions that drag on endlessly. Frequently, project managers spend more time in meetings (although important), than managing the project.

They must therefore also have time management skills (see Figure E.5). Not only must they manage the project's time but their own, too. They must set priorities for their workload to maximize their own productivity. Project managers who work until 10 or 11pm after everyone retires indicate they cannot manage their own time effectively. It may also suggest that they are unable to manage the project effectively.

Project managers must have still another soft skill, that of being effective negotiators (see Figure E.6). They must compete with other project managers for scarce resources, such as people, time, money, equipment, or facilities, and they must fight to acquire what is necessary, proving why they must have the resources that they want. Sometimes the result may mean sharing resources, at other times taking them from another project.

For example, a project manager may be negotiating with a functional manager for an employee. At the same time, other project managers may be competing for the same employee. The project manager must not only negotiate with the func-

- Understand that negotiation is a process, not an event or happening
- Play a poor hand skilfully
- Analyse and understand the other side's position
- Avoid striving for zero-sum results
- Use your power sensibly
- Take calculated risks
- Know your options
- Exude self-confidence
- Determine the other side's power (of legitimacy)
- Share in the overall risk by gaining others' commitment
- Try to gain control over others' behaviour
- Strive for a win–win, not win–lose, result
- Be persistent and persuasive
- Use flexible deadlines
- Do your homework; information is power
- Seek common ground with the other side

Figure E.6   *Guidelines for effective negotiation*

tional manager but also with the other project managers to use the talents of the employee.

In a multi-project computing environment, this competition over people with rare skills and talent can cause havoc with morale and unity within teams and throughout a department. For example, a number of project managers may be competing over a couple of mechanical engineers. Each project manager must negotiate with functional managers and other project managers for the services of these important individuals. Failure to reach an agreement can lower morale and cause dissension over who is supporting whom.

Persuasion skills have a close relationship to effective negotiation skills. Project managers must not only know how to write and speak but in a way that motivates people. Depending on the environment, they may face stiff resistance from all sides. The client may not give the necessary cooperation; senior management may not provide the support, financial or otherwise, to complete the project within time and budget; some team members may not perform to expectations. Overcoming such obstacles requires persuasion.

Decision-making skills are absolutely essential for project managers. They must know what information is required to make a decision and when to make it. They must also be able to analyse the impact of their decisions (see Figure E.7).

Personal characteristics

Hard and soft skills, therefore, are essential, but such skills alone, however, arc insufficient. Project managers must also have certain personal characteristics, which may be innate for some but are more usually acquired through experience. One important characteristic is the ability to see the total picture. Effective project managers recognize that many factors affect the outcome of a project. They consider not only the technical aspects but also others like the economic, personnel, and legal aspects. Their perspective is broad, seeing the whole picture, and requires taking a systems approach.

Many project managers lack this characteristic. They fall into the trap of emphasizing the technical side while neglecting other important areas. As a result, relations with the client may deteriorate; legal complications may arise due to lack of compliance with the contract; and the project team may suffer from high turnover. Reliance solely on the technical aspects often results in a project riddled with problems beyond schedule slides and budget overruns.

Many project managers see their projects as an opportunity to build the product of their dreams. To them other facets of a project are administrivia. Many programmers, for example, become project managers because they are the top COBOL, PL1, or ASSEMBLY language programmers in the organization. They then mistakenly manage the project as if programming were all that mattered.

Organizational ability is another important characteristic. Effective project managers can use available resources and maximize their output. They do that by building a solid organizational structure for their project. They know how and when to delegate; they build effective teams, establish good communication channels, and create an environment that encourages top performance. Without organizational abilities, project managers can quickly lead a project to financial ruin.

Decisiveness is a central characteristic. Some project man-

INDIVIDUAL

STATISTICAL ANALYSIS
REGRESSION ANALYSIS
DESIGN OF EXPERIMENTS
STOCHASTIC PROCESSES
RISK ANALYSIS
VALUE ENGINEERING
LINEAR PROGRAMMING
NON-LINEAR PROGRAMMING
GEOMETRIC PROGRAMMING
TRENDING
PARAMETRICS
CAUSE AND EFFECT
FISHBONE
PSYCHOMETRICS
PROGRAM EVALUATION REVIEW TECHNIQUE
CRITICAL PATH METHOD

TEAM

SIMULATION
ARTIFICIAL INTELLIGENCE
COMPUTER-AIDED SOFTWARE
ENGINEERING (CASE)

BOTH

TRIAL AND ERROR
SCIENTIFIC METHOD
EDUCATED GUESS
RANDOM GUESS
FLIP OF A COIN
FORTUNE TELLING/HOROSCOPE
HINDSIGHT
EXPERIENCE
COMMON SENSE
PASS DECISION TO SOMEONE ELSE

Figure E.7   *Some common decision-making techniques and tools*

agers loathe decision-making and will avoid making one until it is too late or it becomes the wrong one. Even the idea of making a decision paralyzes them, rather like someone standing on a tightrope a thousand feet above the ground. This paralysis can frustrate team members and cause them to lose respect for the project manager. It can also lead to schedule slides, like missing the project completion date.

Some project managers treat their projects like building a product. They need to have 'everything' in place before running with it. Such perfection, although rarely necessary, can lead to indecisiveness due to a failure to make or desire to change decisions. All this indecisiveness results in schedule delay and frustrated team members, clients, and senior managers.

Effective project managers must be decisive but not impulsive, which can lead to negative outcomes. They must make the right decision within a reasonable period of time.

Building a product before defining it is a common example of impulsive decision-making on technical projects. Some project managers purchase highly sophisticated tools to aid productivity before knowing exactly (or relatively nearly) what to provide for the client. In the end, their impulsiveness results in high, unwarranted costs to the project and the client.

Being analytical is a vital characteristic. Effective project managers must identify the source of a problem, whether schedule, cost, or quality. That requires being able to break the problem into parts, looking at the relationships between them, and identifying the source of the problem (as opposed to the symptom). Hence, effective project managers must be good problem identifiers. They can identify a problem, tear it apart, and discover its source.

When project managers discover that their project will not meet the completion date, for example, they must not accuse someone requesting more tools or asking for money unless they are sure of what contributed to the circumstance. They should look for the cause of the schedule delay and address the cause.

In addition, effective project managers must have the ability to solve problems. They must develop a solution and implement it. However, identifying the solution is not enough;

effective project managers must make it happen. That leads to another characteristic, initiative. Effective project managers must have the self-motivation to make the solution a reality. Saying something must be fixed and knowing how to implement it is not enough. Effective project managers make things happen by doing more than pontificate; they must convert talk into reality.

Many project managers need to understand that they are the ones who can make a difference. Simply identifying a problem, such as dealing with an uncooperative client or recognizing poor methods and techniques, does little to improve the outcome of their projects. They must develop and implement solutions and not just list the problems and hope they will go away. They are the ones who must plan, organize, control, and lead their project. No one else can do that.

Effective project managers, furthermore, are proactive, not reactive, people. They do not wait for something to happen; they go out and 'do it'. They do not espouse a managerial style with a laissez-faire quality. They make their decisions and follow through on them. They do not, for example, just put a project plan together and hope that the entire project team follows it. They take direct action to ensure that what does occur is according to their plan.

That requires vision, another characteristic of effective project managers. Indeed, they have an almost innate ability to know where they are going. They have more than an idea. They visualize the idea, giving it definable dimensions.

They are not loners, however, who keep the vision to themselves. Effective project managers inspire others to follow them in transforming the vision into reality. In other words, they must have the ability to inspire others to follow that vision by getting people to perform above, even beyond, expectations.

Another characteristic is integrity. Above all else, effective project managers have integrity. They are honest with all parties – the project team, the client, and senior management. They do not misrepresent anything because losing their integrity means losing credibility. Once credibility is lost, all effectiveness disappears.

The right stuff

Being a project manager is easy. Being an effective one, however, is very difficult. As a project manager, you must plan, organize, control, and lead your project, which involves a host of tasks. Performing those functions and their respective tasks requires the right blend of hard and soft skills. But you must also possess the required characteristics to be 100 per cent effective if you want to develop a quality product, meet schedule dates, and finish within budget.

Glossary

Alliance building: developing a strong relationship with 'friends'

Client: the person(s) or organization(s) who will receive the system being built

Controlling: determining how well a project is progressing according to plans and taking corrective actions, if necessary

Cooption: building alliances with your opponents or 'enemies'

Cost: amount of money spent to perform a task or an entire project

Death: last of the five stages of a project when it is terminated due to lack of support

Decline: fourth of five stages of a project when it goes into a 'winding down' mode and begins to lose its legitimacy

Delegation: assigning a person to perform tasks on your behalf

Disequilibrium: consequence that originates when elements within a system conflict with each other

Divide and conquer: keeping parties competing with one another to maximize your gain or improve your circumstances

Documentation Matrix: a two-dimensional chart showing all project participants and the documentation that they will receive

Esprit de corps: overall morale of a group of people

Feasibility: first of five phases within a project that determines whether the project is a practical alternative to current operations

Filibustering: delaying progress on a project as long as it is to your advantage

Formal power structure: organization that is officially sanctioned by management

Formulation: second of five phases in a project that begins defining in detail what the customer needs and wants and develops alternatives to meet those requirements

Freedom to fail: managerial philosophy that permits the making of one or more mistakes and taking chances without fear of damaging one's career

Freedom to succeed: managerial philosophy that does not permit making mistakes and provides severe consequences for doing so

Gestation: first of five stages of a project that entails its birth

Growth: second of five stages of a project whereby the project earns legitimacy and justifies its existence

Hard skills: expertise that project managers acquire through formal training and experience

Implementation: third of five phases within a project whereby the actual building of the product occurs

Independence: third of five stages of a project when it becomes self-sustaining and has the ability to compete equally with other projects

Informal power structure: organization that is unofficial but 'makes things happen'

Installation: fourth of five phases within a project whereby the product is operational in the client's environment

Leader: person that the project manager selects to assist in managing the project

Leading: motivating people to perform satisfactorily without negative incentives unless absolutely necessary

Matrix organizational structure: individuals from different functional organizations working on a project team while supporting other projects at the same time

Negative incentive: motivating people to perform via threats, castigation, etc.

Network diagram: diagram representing the logical sequence
of tasks to be performed

On the job training: people receiving training at their worksite

Organizational chart: diagram reflecting the reporting relationships among different members of the project team

Organizing: arranging resources in a manner that expedites
the achievement of project goals

Participative management: giving people the opportunity to
participate in the decision-making process

Planning: determining in advance what the project will
achieve

Politics: competition among parties to satisfy needs and wants

Positive incentive: motivating people to perform via induce-
ments

Power broking: playing the 'peacemaker' between two or more
parties competing with one another

Project manager: person with overall responsibility for completing the project successfully

Project team: individuals responsible for building the final
product

Quality: level of workmanship or service that results in an
acceptable product, usually according to the needs of the
customer

Quality assurance: policies, procedures, methods, and activities that address building a product which meets or exceeds
customer requirements and expectations through continuous improvement

Responsibility matrix: two-dimensional chart showing who is
responsible for performing which tasks

Scapegoating: blaming others for one's own problems

Schedule: diagram showing when activities should start and
finish

Senior management: superiors of the project manager

Soft skills: expertise that project managers can acquire but
require considerable application before mastering

Span of control: number of immediate subordinates a person
can effectively manage

Stretching: giving people tasks that challenge them while
encouraging them to do their best

Sustaining: fifth of five phases within a project whereby the client has direct control over the product

Task force: group of people appointed to work on one project only

Unity of command: person reporting to one boss only

Work breakdown structure: listing of tasks to be performed in order to complete the project

Index